What'

America's
HOME COOKING

Illustration by Jan McEvoy

WQED
PITTSBURGH

WQED
PITTSBURGH

For other great merchandise, visit www.ShopWQED.org
or call 1/800-274-1307.
Shop WQED, 4802 Fifth Avenue, Pittsburgh, PA 15213

For WQED Multimedia:

Executive Vice President & Chief Operating Officer
Deborah L. Acklin

Vice President of Business & Finance
Patty Walker

Director of Distribution
Robyn Martin

Distribution Administrator
Hollie Hepler

America's Home Cooking Producer/Host
Chris Fennimore

Graphic Designer
Paula Zetter

Cookbook Editor
Joyce Carr

Table of Contents

WHAT'S FOR DINNER?

Table of Contents

Table of Contents

Table of Contents

WHAT'S FOR DINNER?

America's
HOME COOKING

ON-AIR RECIPES

Alfredo Noodles

DIRECTIONS

Prepare noodles according to package directions. In a large skillet, melt butter. Add cream cheese and garlic, and cook for just 1 minute. Add grated cheese and stir to melt. Slowly add milk, whisking to smooth out any lumps. Season sauce with black pepper. Add pasta to the pan and stir to coat; serve.

INGREDIENTS

1 pound pasta or noodles, any variety

4 tablespoons butter

2 tablespoons cream cheese

2 cloves garlic, finely minced

1 cup grated parmigiano reggiano cheese

1 cup milk

Freshly ground black pepper, to taste

Baked Tilapia

DIRECTIONS

Preheat oven to 350 degrees. Wash filets thoroughly in cold water and be sure there are no bones. Place them in a large bowl in lemon juice and set in the refrigerator for 1 hour.

Drizzle a little olive oil in a 9x13-inch baking pan. Drain lemon juice from fish and add olive oil. Mix gently to coat. Put breadcrumbs in a shallow pan. Coat each filet well on both sides with breadcrumbs and place in the prepared baking pan. Drizzle a little extra olive oil over the top of the fish and sprinkle with the oregano.

Bake for about 30 minutes or until the fish is white and flaky. The tops will often crack open during baking.

INGREDIENTS

2 1/2 pounds tilapia filets

Juice of 1 lemon

1/4 cup olive oil plus more for pan

1 cup flavored breadcrumbs

1 teaspoon oregano

SUBMITTED BY:
Patricia McGrath, Potomac

America's
HOME COOKING

Couscous Pilaf

DIRECTIONS

Heat oil in a saucepan and cook vegetables until soft. Add chicken stock or water and bring to a boil. Stir in couscous. Cover pan and remove it from heat. Set aside for 5 minutes. Fluff with a fork before serving, and sprinkle with toasted pignoli nuts, if desired.

INGREDIENTS

1 tablespoon olive oil

1 small onion, finely diced

1 small carrot, finely diced

1 small celery stalk, finely diced

1/2 teaspoon salt

2 cups chicken stock or water

1 cup couscous

2 tablespoons toasted pignoli nuts (optional)

13

Italian-Style Vegetables

DIRECTIONS

Rinse and trim green beans, broccoli or asparagus into 2-inch pieces. Heat oil in a large skillet. Add onion and stir until soft. Add prosciutto and cook until browned. Add minced garlic and tomato sauce, and bring to a boil. Add vegetable and stir to coat with sauce. Reduce heat to low and cook 5 minutes for green beans, 4 minutes for broccoli or 3 minutes for asparagus.

NOTE

Be careful not to salt this dish before tasting it because the prosciutto will add a lot of saltiness to the dish.

INGREDIENTS

2 pounds green beans, broccoli or asparagus

2 tablespoons olive oil

1 small onion, chopped

4 slices prosciutto, finely diced

1 clove garlic, minced

1 (8-ounce) can tomato sauce

Salt and pepper, to taste

America's
HOME COOKING

Pasta Aglio e Olio

Directions

Heat 2 tablespoons of olive oil in a large skillet over medium heat. Add onion and cook slowly until they start to brown. Add breadcrumbs and stir until brown, about 4 minutes. Set aside.

Cook pasta in 6 quarts of boiling, salted water until al dente.

Heat olive oil in a skillet over medium heat. Add garlic and pepper flakes. When garlic is nicely browned, remove it from pan. Add drained pasta along with 1 cup of boiling liquid. Stir until well coated with oil and then toss with toasted breadcrumbs and parsley.

Ingredients

2 tablespoons olive oil

1 small onion, finely chopped

2 cups breadcrumbs

1 pound spaghetti or linguini

Salt, for boiling water

1/4 cup olive oil

4 cloves garlic, peeled

1/4 teaspoon red pepper flakes

2 tablespoons freshly chopped parsley

Poppy Seed Noodles

DIRECTIONS

Cook pasta according to package directions. In a large skillet, melt butter over medium heat and cook onions until translucent. Add drained pasta and poppy seeds and cook, stirring, until the pasta is well coated and just begins to brown. Sprinkle with minced parsley.

INGREDIENTS

1 pound pasta or egg noodles

3 tablespoons butter

1 small onion, diced

1 tablespoon poppy seeds

2 tablespoons minced fresh parsley

America's
HOME COOKING

Pork Cutlets

DIRECTIONS

Cut pork tenderloin crosswise into 1/2-inch rounds (about 9). Pound pieces gently between sheets of wax paper or plastic wrap until thin. Dredge each piece in flour, dip in beaten eggs and coat with breadcrumbs. If possible, refrigerate cutlets for 1 hour to better adhere breading to the meat before frying.

Heat oil in a skillet over moderate heat; add butter to pan. Fry cutlets a few at a time until golden brown.

Preheat oven to 350 degrees. Prepare a roasting pan by placing a rack in its bottom. Crinkle some aluminum foil on top of the rack. Place cutlets on top of foil (it is okay to stack them if there are a lot). Add about 1/2 to 1 cup water to bottom of the pan. Cover pan tightly with foil and top with pan lid. Bake for about 40 minutes until steamy hot, moist and tender.

Sprinkle cutlets with lemon juice. Serve with applesauce and potato pancakes.

INGREDIENTS

1 (1-pound) pork tenderloin
1/2 cup flour
3 eggs, beaten
1 cup plain breadcrumbs
1/4 cup olive oil
1 tablespoon butter
Water
Juice of 1 lemon

SUBMITTED BY:
Chris Fennimore, WQED Pittsburgh

17

Rice Pilaf

DIRECTIONS

Heat oil in a saucepan. Add onion, carrot and celery and cook until soft. Add rice and stir to coat with oil. Add broth or water and salt, and bring to a boil. Reduce heat to a simmer and cover pan tightly. Simmer for 18 minutes. Remove from heat and fluff with a fork. Sprinkle with toasted pignoli nuts, if desired.

INGREDIENTS

1 tablespoon olive oil

1 small onion, finely diced

1 small carrot, finely diced

1 small celery stalk, finely diced

1 cup long-grain rice

2 cups chicken stock or water

1/2 teaspoon salt

2 tablespoons toasted pignoli nuts (optional)

America's
HOME COOKING

Roasted Root Vegetables

DIRECTIONS

Preheat oven to 375 degrees. Toss all ingredients together in a large mixing bowl. Arrange in a single layer on a cookie sheet with an edge.

Bake for about 30 to 35 minutes, or until vegetables are soft and easily pierced with a fork. Serve immediately.

Serves 4 to 6 with leftovers or 8 to 10 without.

INGREDIENTS

2 to 3 carrots, cut into 1/2-inch pieces

2 to 3 turnips, cut into 1/2-inch pieces

2 beets, cut into 1/2-inch pieces

1 russet potato, cut into 1/2-inch pieces

1 medium red onion, cut into 1/2-inch pieces

3 to 4 cloves garlic, broken open with the flat of a knife

1/4 cup olive oil

Salt and pepper, to taste

SUBMITTED BY:
Chef Jesse Sharrard, CorduroyOrange.com

Sautéed Greens

DIRECTIONS

Wash and trim greens, removing tough stems or spines. Heat oil in a large skillet and add garlic slices. Cook until soft, but not brown. Add greens and stock. Reduce heat to a simmer and cover; cook for 5 minutes for kale or broccoli rabe or 3 minutes for spinach. Remove cover and continue to cook until most of liquid has been absorbed.

INGREDIENTS

1 pound kale, spinach or broccoli rabe

3 tablespoons olive oil

1 large clove garlic, sliced

1/2 cup chicken or vegetable stock

America's
HOME COOKING

Stuffed Chicken Breasts

DIRECTIONS

Make a slit in the side of each chicken breast. Fill slit with 1 slice of ham and 1 piece of asiago cheese. Close slit with tooth picks. Heat oil and butter in a large skillet. Brown chicken breasts on both sides and remove to a warm platter. Sprinkle flour into pan and incorporate with the remaining oil. Cook for about 1 minute. Slowly, add wine and chicken stock, and stir until a smooth sauce forms. Add lemon juice, oregano, salt and pepper. Bring to a boil and return chicken to the pan. Cover pan and reduce heat to a simmer. Simmer for 30 minutes or until chicken is very tender.

INGREDIENTS

4 boneless, skinless chicken breasts

4 slices ham

4 pieces asiago cheese

2 tablespoons olive oil

2 tablespoons butter

3 tablespoons flour

1 cup white wine

1 cup chicken stock

Juice of 1 lemon

1 tablespoon oregano

Salt and pepper, to taste

SUBMITTED BY:
Chris Fennimore, WQED Pittsburgh

WHAT'S FOR DINNER?

America's
HOME COOKING

PROTEIN

40 Garlic Clove Chicken

DIRECTIONS

Preheat oven to 350 degrees. Rinse chicken and pat dry. Season with salt and pepper to taste. Spray a 9x13-inch pan with cooking spray and place chicken in it. Cover chicken with garlic cloves. Add white wine, a little olive oil, chicken broth and seasonings. Bake, covered, for 45 minutes to 1 hour.

When done, remove chicken and garlic. Run garlic through a food chopper. Add garlic puree and pan drippings to a heavy saucepan. Mix flour with white wine or chicken broth. Stir into saucepan. Bring to a boil, stir and cook 1 minute. Spoon over chicken and serve.

INGREDIENTS

1 (3- or 4-pound) chicken, cut up, with skin removed (optional)

Dash salt and pepper

Cooking spray

40 cloves garlic, peeled

2 1/2 cups white wine or chicken broth

Olive oil

1/2 cup chicken broth

1 1/2 teaspoons dried basil, crushed

1 1/2 teaspoons dried oregano, crushed

4 teaspoons all-purpose flour

1/3 cup white wine or chicken broth

SUBMITTED BY:
Terri D. Huska, Hyde Park

Amaretto Shrimp

DIRECTIONS

Melt butter in a skillet until golden brown. Add onions; sauté until transparent. Add shrimp; stir-fry 5 minutes until pink. Add liqueur, almonds and salt; cook 12 minutes until bubbly. Serve in a scallop shell or ramekin and garnish with a sprinkle of chopped parsley.

INGREDIENTS

1/2 cup (1 stick) butter

1 medium onion, finely chopped

1 pound large shrimp, peeled and deveined

1/2 to 1 cup amaretto liqueur

1 cup sliced blanched almonds

1/2 teaspoon salt

Chopped parsley, for garnishing

SUBMITTED BY:
Debbie Chuba, Johnstown

America's
HOME COOKING

Baked Halibut "Plaki"

DIRECTIONS

Preheat oven to 375 degrees. Wash and pat dry steaks; place in lightly oiled baking dish deep enough to hold the vegetable sauce. Squeeze lemon over fish. Bake, uncovered, for 20 minutes. Remove and carefully drain off any liquid that has accumulated. Set aside.

While fish is baking, start vegetable sauce. In large deep pan, heat olive oil. Sauté onion; add garlic to sauté, being careful not to burn it. Add peppers and celery; sauté. Add tomatoes, tomato paste, seasonings and raisins; simmer 5 minutes. Add chopped fresh parsley and spoon over fish. Bake 10 to 15 minutes longer.

NOTE

This is wonderful served with mashed potatoes and good bread with which to gather the sauce. Sauce freezes very well.

INGREDIENTS

4 halibut steaks, about 1 inch thick

Juice of 1 lemon

2 tablespoons olive oil

1 very large Vidalia or sweet onion, sliced medium thick

2 large cloves garlic, minced

1 large red pepper, sliced medium thick

1 cup celery, sliced medium thick

1 (28-ounce) can plum tomatoes, broken up with juices

2 tablespoons tomato paste

Salt and fresh ground pepper, to taste

2 teaspoons dried or fresh Greek oregano

3 teaspoons fresh or dried basil

1/2 cup golden raisins

1/2 cup fresh Italian parsley, chopped

SUBMITTED BY:
Penny Lawrence, Allison Park

Baked Salmon with Creole Mustard Sauce

DIRECTIONS

To make sauce, combine all ingredients except sour cream in a heavy sauce pan. Simmer until thick, about 5 minutes, stirring frequently. This sauce can be prepared a day ahead, covered, refrigerated and then reheated. Just before serving, add sour cream and whisk over low heat. When serving, pass sauce separately.

To cook fish, line a large baking pan with foil. Arrange fish skin-side down in a single layer. Mix butter, sugar, soy sauce, lemon juice and wine in a bowl; pour over fish. Cover and refrigerate at least 1 hour and up to 6 hours. Preheat oven to 400 degrees. Uncover fish and bake until just cooked through, basting occasionally with pan drippings, about 18 minutes.

INGREDIENTS

SAUCE:

1 cup whipping cream

1/4 cup creole mustard

4 teaspoons Worcestershire sauce

1 tablespoon dijon mustard

1/4 teaspoon ground black pepper

1/3 teaspoon ground white pepper

1/3 teaspoon cayenne pepper

2 teaspoons dried basil

1 cup sour cream

FISH:

2 1/2 pounds center-cut salmon fillets

3 cups melted, unsalted butter

3 tablespoons brown sugar

3 tablespoons soy sauce

2 tablespoons fresh lemon juice

2 tablespoons white wine

SUBMITTED BY:
Nancy Polinsky, WQED Pittsburgh

America's
HOME COOKING

Breaded Minute Steaks

DIRECTIONS

Coat steaks with olive oil and press
breadcrumbs onto both sides of each steak.
Cook steaks in broiler for a few minutes on each
side. Let rest for 1 to 2 minutes before serving
to allow juices to settle.

INGREDIENTS

4 minute steaks

2 tablespoons olive oil

1 cup seasoned breadcrumbs

Broiled Salmon Patties

Directions

Combine all ingredients; form into 6
patties. Place foil on broiler rack. Cut slices of
margarine and place on patties. Broil 4 to 5
inches from heat until lightly browned, about 4
or 5 minutes; turn and repeat on other side.

Ingredients

1 (1-pound) can salmon

2 tablespoons onion, minced

2 eggs, beaten

1/4 teaspoon pepper

1/2 teaspoon salt

1/3 cup milk

1/2 cup cracker crumbs

Margarine, for broiling

Submitted by:
Grace and Jane Smith, East Liverpool

America's
HOME COOKING

Chef Tony's Shrimp Scampi

DIRECTIONS

Dredge shrimp in flour lightly. Heat oil and butter in skillet until sizzling. Sauté shrimp over medium-high heat until opaque, about 2 to 4 minutes. Remove to a plate and keep warm. Sauté garlic until lightly colored; add wine and lemon juice, and season with salt and pepper. Simmer 5 to 10 minutes; pour over shrimp.

INGREDIENTS

1 pound raw shrimp, shelled and deveined, with tails on

Flour, for dredging

4 tablespoons olive oil

4 tablespoons (1/2 stick) butter

4 cloves garlic, crushed

1/3 cup white wine

Juice of 1 lemon

Salt and pepper, to taste

SUBMITTED BY:
Benkovitz Seafoods, Pittsburgh

Chicken Croquettes

DIRECTIONS

Melt butter in a medium saucepan. Add flour and whisk to form a roux. Slowly add milk and chicken stock. Simmer, stirring constantly until mixture thickens. Add next 7 ingredients, stir to blend and cool mixture.

Add chicken to mixture and cool. Preheat oven to 375 degrees. Shape mixture into balls the size of tennis balls. Roll in breadcrumbs, and then shape into cones. Dip into egg wash and then into breadcrumbs, carefully maintaining cone shapes. Bake for 20 to 30 minutes.

NOTE

The croquettes can be deep fried in 365-degree oil for 2 1/2 to 3 minutes until golden brown and crispy.

INGREDIENTS

3 tablespoons butter

1/3 cup flour

1/2 cup milk

1/2 cup chicken stock

1 tablespoon chopped parsley

1 teaspoon lemon juice

1 teaspoon grated onion

1/3 teaspoon salt

1/3 teaspoon nutmeg

1/3 teaspoon pepper

Dash paprika

3 cups diced cooked chicken

Breadcrumbs

1 egg and 2 tablespoons water, beaten

Oil, for frying (optional)

SUBMITTED BY:
Bernice and Jim Baran, Pittsburgh

America's
HOME COOKING

Chicken Fingers

DIRECTIONS

Cut chicken into 1/2-inch strips. Place in a large resealable plastic bag. Combine egg, buttermilk and garlic powder. Pour over chicken. Seal and refrigerate for 2 to 4 hours. In another bag, combine flour, breadcrumbs, salt and baking powder. Drain chicken, discarding buttermilk mixture. Put chicken in the bag with flour mixture, seal and shake to coat. Fry chicken until golden brown.

INGREDIENTS

6 boneless, skinless chicken breasts

1 egg, beaten

1 cup buttermilk

1 1/2 teaspoons garlic powder

1 cup flour

1 cup seasoned breadcrumbs

1 teaspoon salt

1 teaspoon baking powder

Oil, for frying

SUBMITTED BY:
Betty Pandullo, Blairsville

Chicken Marengo

DIRECTIONS

Preheat oven to 350 degrees. In a skillet, brown chicken in oil until both sides are brown. Remove to a casserole dish. In the same skillet, sauté onions and garlic, and then add mushrooms. Sauté 3 to 4 minutes, add tomatoes and wine. Season with salt and pepper; simmer for 5 minutes. Add parsley and/or basil. Pour sauce over chicken. Cover and bake for 45 minutes to 1 hour. Serve with rice or noodles. Serves 4 to 6.

INGREDIENTS

2 to 3 chicken breasts, split, boned and skinned

1 onion, sliced

2 garlic cloves, chopped

2 cups sliced mushrooms

1 (16-ounce) can tomatoes, drained and chopped

Salt and pepper, to taste

1/2 cup vermouth or other white wine

Fresh or dried parsley and/or basil

Cooked rice or noodles, for serving

SUBMITTED BY:
Margaret C. Young, Uniontown

America's
HOME COOKING

Chicken Piccata

DIRECTIONS

Dredge chicken in flour mixture. Heat oil in skillet and brown garlic lightly. Remove garlic cloves and discard. Add floured chicken to skillet and sauté on medium heat. As oil begins to cook off, add butter. Sprinkle chicken with lemon juice when cooked through. Remove cooked chicken and add wine to skillet. Stir to form a sauce, which will thicken slightly as it bubbles. Return chicken to skillet for 2 to 3 minutes. Remove chicken to a platter and cover with sauce. Garnish with lemon slices and pepper.

NOTE

This recipe can be prepared with chicken as described or turkey, veal cutlets or pork medallions.

INGREDIENTS

2 chicken breasts, sliced in half horizontally and pounded flat

Flour seasoned with salt, pepper and poultry and fish seasoning, for dredging

1 tablespoon olive oil

4 to 5 cloves garlic, sliced

1 tablespoon butter

Lemon juice

1 to 1 1/2 cups dry white wine

Lemon slices, for garnishing

Black pepper, for garnishing

SUBMITTED BY:
Joe Negri, Pittsburgh

Cod Fish Cakes

Directions

Boil cod fish and shred cooked fish, making sure there are no bones. Boil potatoes, peel and mash potatoes. Add salt and pepper, milk, parsley, cheese, egg and fish. Mix well and form into flattened ball shapes. Roll in breadcrumbs. Fry until golden brown and drain on paper towels.

Ingredients

1 pound cod fish, boned

4 to 6 potatoes

Salt and pepper, to taste

4 tablespoons milk

2 tablespoons chopped parsley

4 tablespoons grated romano cheese

1 egg

1 cup breadcrumbs

Vegetable or canola oil, for frying

SUBMITTED BY:
Chris Fennimore, WQED Pittsburgh

America's
HOME COOKING

Coq au Vin

Directions

Heat butter in a large, high-sided skillet. Dredge chicken pieces in flour until well coated. Brown chicken pieces in butter, browning well on all sides. Add mushrooms, diced ham, minced garlic, thyme, parsley, salt and pepper, and onions. Mix thoroughly and then transfer to a covered casserole dish. Preheat oven to 300 degrees. Heat cognac and pour it over chicken. Ignite the cognac. When the flames die out, add red wine. Cover casserole and bake for 2 1/2 hours.

Ingredients

4 tablespoons (1/2 stick) butter

3 pounds chicken parts, cut in small pieces

Flour, for dredging

1 pound mushrooms

1/3 pound ham slice, diced

1 clove garlic, minced

1 sprig thyme or 1 teaspoon dry

1 sprig parsley or 1 tablespoon dry

Salt and pepper

1 cup small white onions, peeled

1/2 cup cognac

1 cup red wine

Submitted by:
Chris Fennimore, WQED Pittsburgh

Crispy Chicken

DIRECTIONS

Preheat oven to 350 degrees. Wash and dry chicken pieces. Mix mayonnaise and ranch dressing. Dip each piece in mayonnaise mixture and roll in crushed potato chips. Place on a cookie sheet. Sprinkle with garlic powder. Bake for 1 hour.

INGREDIENTS

2 split chicken breasts

4 chicken legs

4 chicken thighs

1/2 cup mayonnaise or salad dressing

1/2 cup ranch dressing

Crushed potato chips

Garlic powder, to taste

SUBMITTED BY:
Gloria McClure, Clarksburg

America's
HOME COOKING

Dilled Shrimp

DIRECTIONS

In a large bowl, mix mayonnaise, lemon juice, sugar, sour cream and dill weed; stir in shrimp. Lay onion rings on top. Cover and refrigerate for several hours. Line a serving plate with lettuce leaves; spoon shrimp mixture over lettuce. Serve immediately. Serves 10.

INGREDIENTS

1 1/2 cups mayonnaise

1/4 cup fresh lemon juice

1/3 cup sugar

1/2 cup sour cream

1 tablespoon fresh dill weed

2 pounds cooked shrimp, shelled and deveined

1 red onion, thinly sliced

Lettuce leaves, for serving

SUBMITTED BY:
Nancy Otto, Indiana

Florida Pork Chops

Directions

Preheat oven to 350 degrees. Heat olive oil in a skillet, and brown chops. Drain well and place in a shallow 9x13-inch casserole dish. Discard oil in skillet and melt butter. Add flour and stir for 1 minute. Gradually add orange juice and wine until well blended. Add brown sugar, orange zest, salt and black pepper. Stir until smooth. Pour sauce over chops and bake for 1 hour.

Note

Chicken can be substituted for pork.

Ingredients

8 pork chops, well trimmed and seasoned with salt and pepper

Olive oil

2 tablespoons butter

2 tablespoons flour

1 1/2 cups orange juice

1/2 cup dry white wine

3 tablespoons brown sugar

1 teaspoon orange zest

1 teaspoon salt

Black pepper, to taste

SUBMITTED BY:
Linda Engbarth Weissert, Pittsburgh

America's
HOME COOKING

Grandma's Chicken Cacciatore

DIRECTIONS

Sauté chicken in oil until lightly browned. Transfer to a roasting pan; set aside. Drain all but 2 tablespoons fat from sauté pan and add onion and garlic. Sauté until onion is transparent. Chop tomatoes and add to pan along with juice from tomatoes, wine, salt, oregano and red pepper flakes. Taste and adjust seasoning if necessary. Bring to a boil; pour sauce over chicken.

Preheat oven to 350 degrees. Cover pan with foil and bake for 30 minutes. Poke holes in foil to release steam and continue baking until chicken is fork tender, about 30 minutes. Serve with crusty Italian bread. Serves 8.

NOTE

This dish also can be served over pasta.

INGREDIENTS

2 (2 1/2- to 3-pound) fryer chickens, cut up

1/3 cup vegetable oil

1 large onion, chopped

2 large garlic cloves, minced

1 (28- or 35-ounce) can plum tomatoes

1/3 cup red or white wine

2 teaspoons salt

1 teaspoon oregano

1/2 to 1 teaspoon crushed hot red pepper

Italian bread, for serving

SUBMITTED BY:
Margie Sciulli, Pittsburgh

41

Hot and Spicy Meatballs

DIRECTIONS

Mix meatball ingredients together thoroughly. Shape into approximately 1/2-inch balls for appetizers or slightly larger for main course. Brown in a skillet in butter; pour off fat. Mix all sauce ingredients in a bowl, and then add to hot skillet in which meatballs were cooked. Add meatballs to sauce, cover and simmer at least 10 minutes.

INGREDIENTS

MEATBALLS:

1 pound ground meat

1 cup soft breadcrumbs

2 tablespoons minced onion

1 tablespoon horseradish

3 drops hot sauce

2 eggs, beaten

1 tablespoon butter, for frying

SAUCE:

1 cup ketchup

1/2 cup water

1/2 cup cider vinegar

2 tablespoons brown sugar

2 teaspoons ground pepper

1 tablespoon minced onion

2 teaspoons Worcestershire sauce

1 teaspoon salt

1 teaspoon dry mustard

3 to 5 drops hot sauce

SUBMITTED BY:
Linda dePaolo

America's
HOME COOKING

Kebobs

INGREDIENTS

DIRECTIONS

In all cases, cut meat and vegetables into 1-inch cubes and place in separate zip-top bags. Add appropriate marinade and marinate overnight or, in the case of the swordfish and shrimp, for 1 hour. Place on metal skewers or soaked wooden skewers and cook over high heat until cooked through and slightly charred on all sides.

SWORDFISH MARINADE:

2 tablespoons canola oil

2 tablespoons lemon juice

1 tablespoon minced dill

SHRIMP MARINADE:

1 tablespoon melted butter

1 tablespoon Worcestershire sauce

1/4 teaspoon Old Bay seasoning

CHICKEN MARINADE:

2 tablespoons olive oil

2 tablespoons balsamic vinegar

1 tablespoon basil

LAMB MARINADE:

1/2 cup plain yogurt

2 tablespoons olive oil

2 tablespoons lemon juice

2 cloves garlic crushed

1 tablespoon coriander

PORK MARINADE:

1 tablespoon olive oil

1 teaspoon toasted sesame oil

2 tablespoons soy sauce

1 clove garlic, crushed

1 tablespoon fresh ginger

Lamb Curry

DIRECTIONS

Heat 1 tablespoon olive oil in a large saucepan and sauté onion and celery until tender, but not brown. Stir in curry powder, salt and flour. Add chicken stock and cook until smooth and thickened. In another pot, heat 2 tablespoons olive oil and cook lamb cubes until nicely browned on all sides and tender. Add curry sauce to lamb and serve over hot rice on a large platter or from a large casserole.

INGREDIENTS

1 tablespoon virgin olive oil

1 onion, finely chopped

1/2 cup finely chopped celery

1 tablespoon curry powder

1/2 teaspoon salt

1/3 cup flour

3 1/2 cups chicken stock

2 tablespoons olive oil

2 1/2 pounds lamb cubes

Hot rice, for serving

SUBMITTED BY:
Elsie Henderson, Pittsburgh

America's
HOME COOKING

Lemon Flounder
with Pine Nuts

Directions

Roll fish in flour, shaking off excess. Heat 2 tablespoons butter in a frying pan. Fry fish on both sides until cooked, turning once. Place on serving dish; keep warm. Clean and dry pan. Heat remaining butter; add pine nuts, lemon juice, parsley and seasonings. Cook until foamy. Pour over fish and sprinkle with extra parsley. Serve with lemon slices. Serves 2.

Ingredients

2 1/2 pounds flounder or sole fillets

Flour, for dredging

4 tablespoons (1/2 stick) butter, divided

2 tablespoons pine nuts

Juice of 1/2 lemon

1 tablespoon fresh parsley

Salt and pepper, to taste

Parsley, for garnishing

Lemon slices, for garnishing

SUBMITTED BY:
Susan Mihalo VanRiper, Allison Park

Little Fuss Tuscan Pork Roast

Directions

Preheat oven to 325 degrees. In a blender, combine garlic, rosemary, oil and salt. Rub all over roast. Cover and let stand for 30 minutes. Place fat-side up on a greased baking rack in a roasting pan. Bake uncovered for 2 to 2 1/2 hours or until internal temperature reaches 160 to 170 degrees. Let stand for 15 minutes before slicing.

Ingredients

5 to 8 garlic cloves, peeled

1 tablespoon dried rosemary

1 tablespoon olive oil

1/2 teaspoon salt

1 (3- to 4-pound) boneless pork loin roast

Submitted by:
Florence Smallwood, Ben Avon

America's
HOME COOKING

Mummy's Apricot Chicken

DIRECTIONS

Preheat oven to 325 degrees. Smear apricot preserves on chicken and place in a baking pan. Pour Russian dressing over chicken, and sprinkle with onion soup mix. Bake for 1 1/2 hours.

INGREDIENTS

1 (2 1/2- or 3-pound) chicken, cut up

1 (10-ounce) jar apricot preserves

1 (8-ounce) bottle Russian dressing

1 (1-ounce) package dry onion soup mix

SUBMITTED BY:
Nancy Polinsky, WQED Pittsburgh

Oven Chicken Paprikash

DIRECTIONS

Preheat oven to 325 degrees. Place onions, garlic and tomatoes in the bottom of a large roasting pan. Season both chickens with salt and pepper. Put chickens in roasting pan, breast side up. Sprinkle with paprika. Pour wine and chicken broth over chickens. Cover tightly and roast for 3 1/2 to 4 hours, or until meat is falling off the bone. (During the last hour of cooking, remove cover to allow chickens to brown.)

When chicken is done, remove large pieces of meat from breast bone and discard all bones. Remove legs and thighs. Stir sour cream into remaining pan juices. Season with salt and pepper. Serves 8.

INGREDIENTS

6 small onions, cut in half

6 whole cloves garlic, peeled

1 (28-ounce) can peeled, diced tomatoes

2 (3- to 4-pound) chickens

Salt and pepper, to taste

1 tablespoon sweet Hungarian paprika

1/2 cup dry wine

1 1/2 cups chicken broth

1 (8-ounce) carton regular or low-fat sour cream

SUBMITTED BY:
Jean Engwer Franks, McKeesport

America's
HOME COOKING

Parmesan-Crusted Fish

DIRECTIONS

Beat egg lightly with garlic powder and pepper; coat fish fillets with beaten egg, draining off excess. Roll fillets in cheese to coat. Let sit 5 minutes before cooking. Heat oils in a large skillet over medium-high heat until hot, but not smoking. Add fish fillets and cook until browned on 1 side, about 2 minutes. Turn fillets over and brown the other side. Sprinkle with parsley and serve with lemon wedges.

INGREDIENTS

1 egg

1/2 teaspoon garlic powder

1/2 teaspoon pepper

2 pounds thin, firm fish fillets, such as orange roughy, red snapper, catfish, etc.

1/2 to 1 cup grated parmesan cheese

1 tablespoon olive oil

1 tablespoon canola oil

2 tablespoons chopped parsley

Lemon wedges, for serving

SUBMITTED BY:
Debbie Chuba, Johnstown

Parmesan Lemon Chicken

DIRECTIONS

Preheat oven to 375 degrees. Wash and dry chicken pieces. Season with salt and pepper. Melt butter. Mix breadcrumbs together with parmesan cheese on a flat plate. Dip chicken pieces in butter then cover with crumb/cheese mixture. Place chicken in a glass 9x13-inch dish. Squeeze lots of lemon juice over chicken pieces. Bake for 45 minutes or until brown and crispy. Place on a serving platter and garnish with lemon slices.

INGREDIENTS

4 whole boneless, skinless chicken breasts, halved

Salt and pepper, to taste

1/2 cup (1 stick) butter

2 cups seasoned breadcrumbs

1 cup grated parmesan cheese

Juice of 4 to 5 lemons

Lemon slices, for garnishing

SUBMITTED BY:
Kathleen Geiger, Pittsburgh

America's
HOME COOKING

Pork Chops with Cranberry

Directions

Preheat oven to 350 degrees. Brown chops very well on both sides in a skillet. Remove to large, shallow baking dish. Combine remaining ingredients except cranberry sauce and heat in a saucepan until sugar dissolves. Add sauce and heat. Pour over chops and cover dish with foil. Bake for about 45 minutes.

Ingredients

8 pork chops
3 tablespoons sugar
1 teaspoon cinnamon
1/2 teaspoon nutmeg
1/2 tablespoon cloves
1/2 cup port wine
1 cup cranberry sauce

Submitted by:
Ginny Griffin, Moon Township

51

Pork Medallions Piccata

DIRECTIONS

Slice pork into 1/2-inch medallion slices. Flatten each slice between waxed paper to 1/2 inch thick. In a pie plate, combine flour and lemon pepper. Dredge pork slices in flour mixture. In a large skillet, melt margarine and sauté medallions 5 to 6 minutes, turning once. Add wine and lemon juice. Shake pan gently and cook 2 to 3 minutes or until sauce is slightly thickened. This dish can be garnished with lemon slices, chopped parsley and capers. Serves 4.

INGREDIENTS

1 (1- or 1 1/2-pound) boneless pork tenderloin

2 tablespoons all-purpose flour

1 1/2 teaspoons lemon pepper

2 tablespoons margarine

1/2 cup dry sherry wine

2 to 3 tablespoons fresh lemon juice

SUBMITTED BY:
Deborah Martin, Bethel Park

America's
HOME COOKING

Shashlyk

DIRECTIONS

Remove bone and skin from lamb and cut off excess fat. Cut meat into 1x2-inch pieces and put in a bowl. Combine remaining ingredients, pour over the meat and mix thoroughly. Cover and let mixture stand for 2 hours or longer at room temperature to marinate and tenderize meat.

Arrange meat cubes on a skewer. Brush filled skewers very generously with cooking oil. Place skewers under the broiler close to strong heat. Turn skewers every few minutes and baste frequently with olive oil. Total broiling time is about 12 minutes. Serve immediately.

NOTE

Pork or beef may be substituted or used in conjunction with lamb.

INGREDIENTS

2 to 3 pounds leg of lamb
1/2 cup olive oil
1/2 cup vinegar
1/2 cup water
1/2 cup red wine
1 large onion, chopped
1 clove garlic, crushed
10 peppercorns
1/2 bay leaf
1/2 teaspoon salt

Stewed Cod

DIRECTIONS

Cut cod into 4 pieces. In a 9- or 10-inch skillet, heat olive oil over medium heat. Add garlic and cook until soft. Stir in tomato soup and water; add cheese. Blend ingredients; add cod, salt and pepper. Cover and cook over low heat; take lid off twice while cooking and baste fish by spooning tomato soup sauce over it. Cook until fish flakes easily with a fork; let rest for about 15 minutes. Serves 4.

INGREDIENTS

1 pound fresh or frozen and slightly thawed cod

2 tablespoons olive oil

2 or 3 garlic cloves, diced

1 (10 1/2-ounce) can tomato soup

2 cups water

3 tablespoons romano cheese, grated

Salt and pepper, to taste

SUBMITTED BY:
Charlotte K. Wertz, Pittsburgh

America's
HOME COOKING

Texas-Style Chicken-Fried Steak with Cream Gravy

DIRECTIONS

Cut steak into 4 pieces and pound to tenderize. Combine flour, salt and pepper.

In a heavy skillet, heat 1/2 inch of oil. Dip each piece of steak in flour mixture, then into evaporated milk and into flour mixture again. Fry in oil over medium-high heat until lightly browned. Remove and drain on paper towels.

After frying chicken-fried steak, pour off all but 3 tablespoons oil from the pan. Loosen any browned pieces from pan bottom and add flour. Combine evaporated milk and water. With pan over medium heat, gradually add milk and water mixture, stirring constantly until thickened. Scrape sides and bottom to loosen any more browned pieces. Season to taste with salt and pepper.

Serve steak with gravy. Serves 4.

INGREDIENTS

1 pound round steak

1 cup flour

1 teaspoon salt

1/2 teaspoon pepper

Oil, for frying

1/2 cup evaporated milk

CREAM GRAVY:

3 tablespoons pan drippings

3 tablespoons flour

1 cup evaporated milk

1 cup water

Salt and pepper, to taste

SUBMITTED BY:
Frances Gibson, Pittsburgh

55

Trout Almondine

DIRECTIONS

Preheat oven to 400 degrees. Sauté mushrooms. Stuff trout with almonds, mushrooms and breadcrumbs. Drizzle inside of fish with 1/4 cup almond liqueur. Top fish with remaining liqueur and almonds.

Bake 10 to 15 minutes or until flaky.

INGREDIENTS

1/2 cup mushrooms

1 fresh trout, cleaned

1 cup sliced blanched almonds, to taste

1/2 cup plain breadcrumbs

1/2 cup almond liqueur, to taste

SUBMITTED BY:
Bridget Sluka, Greensburg

America's
HOME COOKING

Veal, Pork or Chicken Scaloppini

DIRECTIONS

Cut and pound meat into 3x3-inch slices that are approximately 1/4 inch thick. Dredge pieces in flour. Heat butter in a large skillet and sauté mushrooms until they give up their liquid; remove to a dish. Add 2 tablespoons olive oil to the skillet and fry meat pieces until golden brown. Remove to a platter. Add remaining olive oil and sauté onion and garlic until soft, but not brown. Season with spices and add wine or stock. Return meat and mushrooms to pan. Reduce to a simmer and cook, covered, for about 10 minutes.

INGREDIENTS

2 pounds veal, chicken breasts or pork tenderloin

1 cup flour

2 tablespoons butter

1 pound mushrooms, sliced

3 tablespoons olive oil, divided

1 onion, chopped

1 clove garlic, crushed

1/4 teaspoon oregano

1/4 teaspoon basil

1/2 teaspoon parsley

Salt and pepper, to taste

1 cup dry white wine or stock

WHAT'S FOR DINNER?

America's
HOME COOKING

VEGTABLES

Asparagus/Apple Salad

DIRECTIONS

Steam asparagus 2 to 3 minutes, cool. Combine with apples and eggs. Mix dressing ingredients well; add dressing to salad. Let marinate at least 1 hour in refrigerator. Serve on cut-up greens.

INGREDIENTS

2 cups asparagus, cut in 1-inch pieces

1 cup diced red apple

2 hard-boiled eggs, diced

Cut-up greens, for serving

DRESSING:

4 tablespoons vinegar

4 tablespoons olive oil

4 tablespoons honey

4 tablespoons minced parsley

SUBMITTED BY:
Martha Howard, Morgantown

Asparagus Casserole

DIRECTIONS

Preheat oven to 375 degrees. Mix cracker crumbs with 1/2 pound melted butter. Make white sauce using 4 tablespoons butter, flour, salt and pepper, milk and cheese. Line the bottom of a 2-quart casserole with half of the crumb mixture. Arrange well-drained asparagus on top of crumb mixture. Sprinkle with almonds. Cover with white sauce. Bake for 30 minutes.

INGREDIENTS

1 1/2 cups butter cracker crumbs

1/2 pound melted butter or margarine plus 4 tablespoons butter, divided

3 tablespoons flour

Salt and pepper, to taste

1 1/2 cups milk

1 (5-ounce) jar old English cheese spread

2 (15-ounce) cans asparagus spears, well-drained, or 1 pound fresh asparagus, freshly cooked and well-drained

1/2 cup slivered almonds

SUBMITTED BY:
Faye Cohen, Mt. Lebanon

America's
HOME COOKING

Asparagus Chinese Style

Directions

Cut asparagus diagonally in very thin slices. Heat stock to boiling and stir in cornstarch, water and soy sauce. Stirring constantly, cook until thickens. Add garlic, salt and pepper. Sauté sliced asparagus in hot oil for 2 minutes. Pour sauce over asparagus and stir constantly. Cook 1 minute longer. Serve hot.

Ingredients

2 pounds fresh asparagus

1/2 cup chicken stock

1 tablespoon cornstarch

1 tablespoon cold water

2 tablespoons soy sauce

1 garlic clove, minced

Salt and pepper, to taste

2 tablespoons olive oil

Submitted by:
Kimi Takahashi, Point Breeze

Asparagus Forester

Directions

Steam asparagus until crisp-tender. In a medium skillet, melt butter over medium-high heat. Add shallots. Cook until soft, about 3 to 5 minutes. Add mushrooms and cook, stirring often, until soft. Stir in sour cream, brown mustard, salt and pepper. Cook until just heated through. Do not boil sauce. Serve sauce over asparagus. Serves 6.

Ingredients

1 1/2 pounds fresh asparagus

2 tablespoons butter or margarine

2 tablespoons shallots, finely chopped

2 cups mushrooms, sliced

1/2 cup sour cream

2 teaspoons prepared brown mustard

1/4 teaspoon salt

1/4 teaspoon pepper

Submitted by:
Christina R. Bradley, *Three Rivers Cookbook III*

America's
HOME COOKING

Asparagus in Puff Pastry with Lemon Sauce

DIRECTIONS

Trim tough ends of asparagus and peel stalks. Cook for 3 minutes in a pan of boiling water and then shock asparagus in a bowl of ice water to stop cooking and retain a deep green color.

Preheat oven to 400 degrees.

Divide puff pastry into 8 rectangles. Place 1/4 of asparagus on 1 puff pastry rectangles. Top with 1 ounce goat cheese and a sprinkling of salt and pepper. Wet edges of rectangle with water and place a second sheet on top, leaving asparagus tips exposed. Press edges to seal and trim any excess. Repeat with remaining pastry and asparagus. Place bundles on a parchment-lined baking sheet and bake for 12 to 15 minutes or until the pastry is nicely browned.

Melt butter in a small saucepan. Stir in flour and cook slowly for 3 minutes. Mix in wine and lemon juice and season with salt and pepper. Stir until thickened. Serve with asparagus bundles. Serves 4.

INGREDIENTS

1 pound asparagus
1 (17-ounce) package puff pastry
4 ounces goat cheese
Salt and pepper, to taste

SAUCE:
2 tablespoons butter
2 tablespoons flour
1 cup white wine
Juice of 1 lemon
Salt and pepper, to taste

Asparagus Salad

Directions

In a shallow container, spread out asparagus. Mix all dressing ingredients in a jar; shake vigorously. Pour dressing over asparagus. Chill overnight.

Ingredients

1/2 to 1 pound freshly steamed, 2-inch asparagus pieces

Dressing:

1/2 cup salad oil

2 tablespoons vinegar

2 tablespoons lemon juice

2 teaspoons sugar

2 teaspoons salt

1/2 teaspoon paprika

1/2 teaspoon dry mustard

Dash cayenne pepper

2 tablespoons chopped pimento-stuffed green olives

1 hard-boiled egg, chopped

2 plum tomatoes, diced

Submitted by:
Heidi Souza, Moon Township

America's
HOME COOKING

Asparagus Sautéed with Prosciutto and Garlic

Directions

Trim and peel asparagus and cut on the bias into 2-inch pieces. Cook prosciutto in a skillet until it starts to crisp. Add garlic and asparagus and sauté until asparagus is crisp-tender. Season with black pepper (salt is unnecessary) and serve. Serves 4.

Ingredients

1 pound asparagus

1/8 pound prosciutto, finely diced

1 clove garlic, minced

Fresh black pepper

Baked Green Tomatoes

DIRECTIONS

Preheat oven to 350 degrees. Cut tomatoes slightly less than 1/2 inch thick and arrange half in a single layer on a greased baking dish. Spread half of bread cubes on top of tomatoes. Season with salt and pepper, and dot with half of margarine. Repeat process, making a second layer. Sprinkle cheese on top. Bake, uncovered, for 45 to 50 minutes or until tender. Serves 6.

INGREDIENTS

8 medium green tomatoes

1 cup small bread cubes, toasted

1 1/2 teaspoons salt

1/8 teaspoon pepper

3 tablespoons margarine

1/3 cup grated parmesan cheese

SUBMITTED BY:
Lola Olinski, Maynard

America's
HOME COOKING

Baked Mushroom Casserole

Directions

Preheat oven to 350 degrees. Sauté onion and mushrooms in butter or margarine for 4 to 5 minutes. Combine remaining ingredients in a bowl. Add to onion/mushroom mixture. Mix well and pour into a greased 1 1/2-quart casserole dish. Bake for 30 minutes, covered. Remove cover and bake for another 30 minutes. Let rest for 5 minutes before serving.

Note

This dish is great served with any type of meat, chicken or fish. It is also a good side dish and good the "second time around." Always refrigerate the leftovers.

Ingredients

1 large onion, chopped

1 pound fresh mushrooms, sliced, or 4 (4-ounce) cans sliced mushrooms, drained

1/4 cup butter or margarine

1 cup cracker crumbs

2 eggs, beaten

1/2 cup cream

1/2 teaspoon salt

4 ounces cheddar or other cheese, shredded

Submitted by:
Frank Hilliard, East Liverpool

69

Braised Kale

Directions

Wash kale thoroughly. Remove stems and finely chop. Cut or tear leaves into bite-sized pieces. Dice bacon and sauté slowly in a large Dutch oven until crisp. Add garlic and cook for just 1 minute before adding kale to pot. (Kale will cook down considerably.) Once kale is wilted, add chicken stock and spices. Cover and let simmer for about 20 minutes, stirring occasionally. Kale is done when stem pieces are tender.

Ingredients

1 large bunch kale, about 2 to 3 pounds

4 slices bacon

2 cloves garlic, minced

1 cup chicken stock

Salt and pepper, to taste

Red pepper flakes, to taste

America's
HOME COOKING

Broccoli and Asparagus Salad

DIRECTIONS

Mix together all ingredients for the salad except for lettuce and egg. Place lettuce leaves on a plate and place salad on lettuce leaves. In a separate bowl, mix ranch dressing and dijon mustard to taste. Drizzle dressing over salad. Garnish with eggs and cracked black pepper.

INGREDIENTS

SALAD:

3 cups steamed broccoli, cooled, chopped and drained well

1 cup steamed asparagus spears, cooled and cut into 1-inch pieces

1 cup marinated artichoke hearts or marinated mushrooms

1 red onion, very thinly sliced

1/2 cup cheese, such as feta, farmers or gorgonzola

Lettuce leaves or hearts of lettuce

2 hard-boiled eggs, cooled and sliced, for garnishing

Cracked black pepper, for garnishing

DRESSING:

Ranch dressing

Dijon mustard

SUBMITTED BY:
Teresa Manning, Pittsburgh

Broccoli Bake

DIRECTIONS

Cook broccoli and drain well. Preheat oven to 350 degrees. Add margarine, salt and pepper. Beat eggs; add breadcrumbs, mushrooms and pimentos. Place into greased 9x13-inch dish, and top with more breadcrumbs and paprika. Bake for 30 minutes.

INGREDIENTS

2 (10-ounce) packages chopped broccoli

2 tablespoons margarine

Salt and pepper, to taste

2 eggs

1/4 cup plain or seasoned breadcrumbs

1 (4-ounce) can mushrooms

1 (4-ounce) jar diced pimentos

SUBMITTED BY:
Catherine Monte Carlo, Monongahela

America's
HOME COOKING

Broccoli Cheese Casserole

DIRECTIONS

Boil broccoli and drain. Sauté onions and mushrooms in butter. Stir in soup, cheddar cheese and milk. Once sauce becomes smooth, stir in broccoli.

INGREDIENTS

1 (16-ounce) bag frozen broccoli

1 small onion, chopped

1 cup sliced fresh mushrooms

1 teaspoon butter

1 (10 1/2-ounce) can cream of mushroom soup

1 (5-ounce) jar old English cheese spread

1/4 cup milk

SUBMITTED BY:
Barbara Woneldorf, Apollo

Broccoli Salad

DIRECTIONS

Cut broccoli into florets. Peel and slice stem into 1/4-inch pieces. Drop broccoli into boiling water for 2 minutes. Drain and chill in ice water, and then drain again. Fry bacon until crisp, drain on paper towels until cool and crumble. In a large bowl, mix mayonnaise, vinegar and sugar, and then toss in the other ingredients to coat.

INGREDIENTS

2 bunches broccoli

1/2 pound bacon (optional)

1 cup shredded part-skim mozzarella cheese

1 cup mayonnaise

2 tablespoons cider vinegar

1/2 cup sugar

1 red pepper, cut in 1/4x1-inch strips

NOTE

You can make a healthier version of this salad by eliminating the bacon and substituting plain yogurt for mayonnaise. The most important thing is not to overcook the broccoli, which should be crisp and not limp.

America's
HOME COOKING

Broccoli Soufflé Baked in Tomatoes

DIRECTIONS

Slice 1/2 inch off top of each tomato, then scoop out insides with sharp spoon. Sprinkle insides with salt. Invert over paper towels and let drain 20 minutes. Spray 10-inch nonstick skillet with nonstick cooking spray. Set over medium-high heat and add oil. When oil is hot, add onions, broccoli stems and florets, and sauté 5 minutes. Spoon vegetables onto side plate.

Add flour to skillet and cook, whisking for 2 minutes. Whisk in milk and simmer 5 minutes until sauce is thick. Remove from heat. Add vegetables, cheese, egg, chives and thyme. Preheat oven to 400 degrees. In clean bowl, beat egg whites until stiff peaks form. Fold into vegetables. Spoon mixture into tomato shells, mounding slightly on top. Place stuffed tomatoes cut-side up in large oiled baking dish. Bake for 15 to 20 minutes. Serves 8.

INGREDIENTS

8 medium ripe, firm tomatoes

1/2 teaspoon salt

1 teaspoon olive oil

2 tablespoons minced onions

1/4 cup minced broccoli stems

1/2 cup broccoli florets

1 tablespoon flour

1/3 cup nonfat milk

3/4 cup shredded part-skim mozzarella cheese

1 large egg

3 tablespoons minced fresh chives

1/2 teaspoon dried thyme

2 egg whites

SUBMITTED BY:
Eleanor M. Bamonte, Natrona Heights

Broccoli Tomato Casserole

DIRECTIONS

Arrange broccoli in a 10-inch round, buttered casserole. Top with tomato slices. Combine mayonnaise and parmesan cheese, reserving a little cheese to sprinkle on top. Spread mayonnaise mixture over tomato slices and sprinkle with reserved cheese. Cover and refrigerate until ready to bake. Preheat oven to 325 degrees. Bake casserole, uncovered, 50 to 60 minutes or until nicely browned.

INGREDIENTS

3 (10-ounce) packages frozen broccoli, thawed and drained

3 large tomatoes, about 1 quart, peeled and sliced

2 cups mayonnaise

2/3 cups grated parmesan cheese

SUBMITTED BY:
Charlene Kula, Greensburg

Broccoli-Tomato Salad

DIRECTIONS

In a large salad bowl, combine broccoli, cauliflower, bacon, onion, tomatoes and eggs; set aside. In another bowl, combine mayonnaise, sugar and vinegar; mix until smooth. Just before serving, pour dressing over salad and toss. Serves 6 to 8.

INGREDIENTS

1 bunch broccoli, separated into florets

1 head cauliflower, separated into florets

8 bacon strips, fried and crumbled

1/3 cup chopped onion

1 cup tomatoes, seeded and chopped

2 hard-cooked eggs, sliced

1 cup mayonnaise or salad dressing

1/3 cup sugar

2 tablespoons vinegar

SUBMITTED BY:
Lola Olinski, Maynard

Carrot Salad

Directions

Grate carrots using the coarse side of a grater, and toss together all ingredients, except sunflower seeds, and let them marinate to mix flavors. Sprinkle sunflower seeds on just before serving to retain crunchiness.

Ingredients

2 pounds carrots, grated

1 cup golden raisins

4 tablespoons orange juice concentrate

4 tablespoons mayonnaise

2 (8-ounce) cans crushed pineapple, drained

1/2 cup shredded coconut

1/2 cup roasted sunflower seeds

America's
HOME COOKING

Cheddar-Almond-Broccoli Casserole

DIRECTIONS

Preheat oven to 375 degrees. Wash and cut broccoli into spears. In a large saucepan, bring 1 inch of water to a boil. Add broccoli and salt. Cook covered for 8 to 12 minutes or until crisp-tender. Drain broccoli and transfer to a 2-quart rectangular or oval baking dish. Meanwhile, in a medium saucepan over medium heat, melt butter and blend in flour. Then add milk, water and bouillon. Cook and stir until thickened and bubbly. Add lemon juice, sherry and pepper. Pour sauce over broccoli. Sprinkle with cheddar cheese and almonds. Bake, uncovered, for 15 to 20 minutes or until bubbly.

INGREDIENTS

1 1/2 pounds broccoli or 2 (10-ounce) packages frozen broccoli spears

1/2 teaspoon salt

1/4 cup butter

1/4 cup flour

1 cup skim milk

3/4 cup water

1 teaspoon instant chicken or beef bouillon granules

Juice of 1 lemon

1 tablespoon dry sherry

1/8 teaspoon pepper

1/2 cup shredded cheddar cheese

1/4 cup toasted sliced almonds

SUBMITTED BY:
Mary E. Barilla, Steubenville

Crunchy Fried Tomatoes

DIRECTIONS

Wash tomatoes; cut into 3/4-inch slices. Dip slices into egg and then roll in breadcrumbs. Melt margarine in large skillet. Add tomato slices; cook until golden brown, turning once. Season tomatoes with salt and pepper, to taste.

INGREDIENTS

4 green medium tomatoes

1 egg, beaten

1 cup dry breadcrumbs

1/3 cup margarine

Salt and pepper, to taste

SUBMITTED BY:
Lola Olinski, Maynard

America's
HOME COOKING

Easy Hollandaise Sauce

DIRECTIONS

Melt butter in a small saucepan over low heat until bubbling. Place egg yolks, water, lemon juice and peppers in a blender. Blend at high speed until smooth. Immediately add hot butter in a steady stream. Stop blender.

NOTE

This sauce is delicious served on top of cooked asparagus garnished with pimento slices.

INGREDIENTS

3/4 pound butter (no substitutions)

4 egg yolks

2 tablespoons water

1/2 teaspoon fresh lemon juice

Dash ground white pepper

Dash ground cayenne pepper

SUBMITTED BY:
Mary Roberge, Pittsburgh

Eggplant Casserole

DIRECTIONS

Slice eggplant with skin on, then cut into 1-inch cubes. Cook in boiling water until eggplant is fairly soft, about 15 minutes. In a skillet, cook bacon until brown and break into 1-inch pieces, or slice bacon into 1-inch strips before cooking. Drain off most of bacon grease, leaving enough to sauté onions. Place eggplant, sautéed onions and bacon into ungreased casserole dish.

Preheat oven to 350 degrees. Cut up tomatoes, reserving juice. Add tomatoes and reserved juice to casserole. Break bread up into small pieces and mix into casserole. (The bread soaks up a little of the juice.) Add enough shredded cheese to cover casserole. Bake for 30 minutes or until casserole and cheese are bubbly.

INGREDIENTS

1 large eggplant

1 pound or 8 ounces regular, low-sodium or low-fat bacon

1 medium or large yellow onion, sliced and cut into small pieces

1 (5-ounce) can whole tomatoes

2 to 3 slices whole wheat bread

Medium or sharp cheddar cheese, shredded

NOTE

This dish can be used as a main dish with salad and baked potatoes or rice or as a side dish with chicken, fish or pork.

SUBMITTED BY:
Diane Mercer, Pittsburgh

America's
HOME COOKING

Eggplant Meatballs
(Polpetti di Melanzane)

DIRECTIONS

Wash eggplant; cut off ends, peel and then cut into chunks. Boil in salted water until soft. Drain well; remove water from eggplant by carefully squeezing. In a large mixing bowl, combine eggplant with remaining ingredients, except olive oil; mix well. Refrigerate covered for several hours or overnight. Form mixture into 1-inch balls. Roll balls in additional Italian breadcrumbs and fry in olive oil until crusty. Drain on brown paper bags. Serve as is or cover with tomato sauce and grated cheese.

NOTE

It may be necessary to add additional crumbs to the mixture if it does not form balls easily.

INGREDIENTS

2 large eggplants, about 4 pounds

2 cups Italian breadcrumbs

1/4 cup chopped fresh parsley

3 minced garlic cloves

2 large eggs

1 1/2 cups grated romano or parmesan cheese

Olive oil, for frying

SUBMITTED BY:
Barbara Vaglia McCalley, McCandless Township

English Walnut Broccoli

DIRECTIONS

Cook broccoli in salted water until tender, drain and turn into greased 1 1/2-quart rectangular casserole. Preheat oven to 350 degrees. In a saucepan, melt 1/2 cup butter, whisk in flour and chicken base or cubes, stirring to make a smooth paste (roux). Gradually add milk; cook and stir until thick and smooth. Pour sauce evenly over broccoli. Heat water and 6 tablespoons butter until butter melts. Pour over stuffing mix and toss to coat. Add walnuts to stuffing and toss again. Top broccoli and sauce with stuffing mix. Bake for 30 minutes. Serves 8.

INGREDIENTS

2 (10-ounce) packages frozen chopped broccoli

1/2 cup butter

4 tablespoons flour

1 1/2 tablespoons chicken base or 4 crushed bouillon cubes

2 cups milk

2/3 cup water

6 tablespoons butter

2/3 (8-ounce) package herb stuffing mix

2/3 cup coarsely chopped walnuts

SUBMITTED BY:
Bill Russell, Beaver

America's
HOME COOKING

Fire and Ice Tomatoes

Directions

In a large bowl, combine tomatoes, onion, green pepper and cucumber. In a small saucepan, combine vinegar, water, sugar, celery salt, mustard seed, salt, cayenne pepper and black pepper. Bring to a boil over medium-high heat; boil for 1 minute. Pour hot vinegar mixture over vegetables. Cover and refrigerate 8 hours or overnight to let flavors blend. Serve with a slotted spoon.

Ingredients

6 medium tomatoes, peeled and quartered

1 medium onion, sliced

1 medium green bell pepper, cut into strips

1 large cucumber, peeled and sliced

3/4 cup cider vinegar

1/4 cup water

1 tablespoon plus 2 teaspoons granulated sugar

1 1/2 teaspoons celery salt

1 1/2 teaspoons mustard seed

1/4 teaspoon salt

1/2 teaspoon cayenne pepper

1/8 teaspoon black pepper

Submitted by:
Charlene Kula, Greensburg

Fried Green Tomatoes

Directions

Wash tomatoes and pat dry. Slice into 1/2-inch slices. Combine flour, cornmeal, salt, pepper and garlic powder. Place in a shallow bowl or plate. Heat oil or shortening in a frying pan. Coat each slice with flour mixture and shake off excess flour. Place into the hot pan and brown on both sides. After tomatoes are brown, reduce heat and partially cover pan. Cook until the tomatoes are tender.

To make a cream sauce, remove tomatoes from pan; add a little cream to pan and heat until thickened. Serve along side of the tomatoes. Serves 6 to 8.

Ingredients

6 to 8 large green tomatoes

1/2 cup flour

1/2 cup cornmeal

2 teaspoons salt

1 teaspoon black pepper

1/2 teaspoons garlic powder (optional)

1/2 cup cooking oil or shortening

Heavy cream, for sauce

Submitted by:
Carolyn Moschak, Pittsburgh (recipe from Oleta Steele, Grand Prairie)

America's
HOME COOKING

Harvest Vegetable Salad

Directions

Combine vegetables in a large bowl. Beat mustard, vinegar, garlic and wine together with a wire whisk. Add oil a few drops at a time and whisk together. Season dressing with salt and pepper. Add tarragon leaves to vegetables. Pour dressing over all and toss.

Serves 24.

Note

Pasta can be added to make a heartier dish, but dressing must be doubled to cover all of the salad.

Ingredients

3 pounds carrots, julienned

3 pounds zucchini, cut into rounds

2 pounds fresh mushrooms, sliced

4 large sweet red peppers, cut into strips

5 cucumbers, sliced

4 pints cherry tomatoes, halved

24 radishes, sliced

1 large head cauliflower, cut into florets

Dressing:

3 tablespoons dijon mustard

1/2 cup red wine vinegar

3 cloves garlic, crushed

1/4 cup cabernet wine

1 cup olive oil

Fresh tarragon leaves

Salt and pepper, to taste

Submitted by:
Susan Mihalo VanRiper, Allison Park

Korean-Style Asparagus

DIRECTIONS

Snap off woody ends of asparagus. Cut stalks on the diagonal into 1-inch pieces.

Heat sesame oil in a medium-size skillet or wok. Add asparagus and stir-fry over high heat for 1 minute. Add soy sauce and broth. Cover and simmer at low heat for 5 minutes.

Remove asparagus to a serving dish. Reduce leftover sauce in the skillet, pour over asparagus and sprinkle with pine nuts.

INGREDIENTS

1 pound fresh asparagus

2 tablespoons sesame oil

2 tablespoons soy sauce

1/2 cup chicken broth

2 tablespoons chopped, toasted pine nuts

SUBMITTED BY:
Debbie Chuba, Johnstown

America's
HOME COOKING

Marinated Mushrooms and Vegetables

DIRECTIONS

Combine first 9 ingredients (vinegar through pepper) in a saucepan. Bring to a boil and simmer uncovered for 10 minutes. In a bowl, combine remaining ingredients. Pour hot marinade over vegetables. Cover and chill. Drain to serve.

INGREDIENTS

2/3 cup vinegar

2/3 cup oil

1/4 cup chopped onions

2 cloves garlic, minced

1 teaspoon sugar

1 teaspoon dried basil

1 teaspoon dried oregano

1 teaspoon salt

1/4 teaspoon pepper

1/2 pound mushrooms, quartered

1 (16-ounce) can tiny carrots

1 cup pitted black olives, halved

1 cup sliced celery

1 (2-ounce) jar pimentos, drained and chopped

SUBMITTED BY:
Marion Stewart, Pittsburgh

Mediterranean Tomato Salad

DIRECTIONS

Halve garlic and rub a large salad bowl with the cut side. Discard garlic. Combine tomatoes, olives and cheese in salad bowl. Add vinegar, oil, oregano and thyme; toss to mix well. Season with salt and pepper.

Cover and refrigerate at least 4 hours to let flavors blend. Let salad stand at room temperature 1 or 2 hours before serving.

NOTE

If desired, drain some of the dressing before serving. Thoroughly drain leftovers before storing in the refrigerator.

INGREDIENTS

1 clove garlic

3 large ripe tomatoes, cut into bite-size pieces

12 pitted black olives, halved

3/4 cup cubed feta cheese

3 tablespoons red wine vinegar

1/2 cup olive oil

1/2 teaspoon dried oregano

1/2 teaspoon dried thyme

Salt, to taste

Freshly ground black pepper, to taste

SUBMITTED BY:
Charlene Kula, Greensburg

America's
HOME COOKING

Mom's Zucchini Casserole

DIRECTIONS

Preheat oven to 350 degrees. Spray a rectangular baking dish with cooking spray or grease the bottom with butter or oil. Begin layering—zucchini layer on the bottom, followed by a layer of tomatoes and ending with cheese slices. Sprinkle dish with breadcrumbs and then lightly sprinkle with seasonings. Repeat layers until top of dish is reached or vegetables run out. The final layer will be parsley sprinkled on top. Cover with foil and bake for 30 minutes. Remove foil and bake an additional 10 to 15 minutes, or until cooked through.

INGREDIENTS

2 large zucchinis, sliced about 1/4 inch thick

3 large tomatoes, sliced about 1/4 inch thick

16 ounces mozzarella cheese, sliced

2 cups breadcrumbs

Garlic powder, to taste

Onion powder, to taste

Celery salt, to taste

Salt and pepper, to taste

Chopped parsley, to taste

SUBMITTED BY:
Karen Lee Puchnick, Butler

Nanna's Eggplant Patties

DIRECTIONS

Cut eggplant into small unpeeled cubes, steam until tender, drain, cool and squeeze out water. Combine with all other ingredients, mix well and form into small patties. Fry in vegetable or olive oil until golden brown.

NOTE

These are also known as vegetarian burgers or black cookies.

INGREDIENTS

1 large (2-pound) eggplant

1/2 cup fresh chopped basil

1 cup breadcrumbs

1/2 teaspoon salt

1/4 teaspoon pepper

1/4 teaspoon garlic powder

1/2 cup grated parmesan cheese

1 large egg, beaten

Vegetable or olive oil, for frying

SUBMITTED BY:
Marianne Cascone-Hilty, Arnold

America's
HOME COOKING

Plum Tomato Tart

DIRECTIONS

Set oven rack on upper level and preheat to 400 degrees. Lightly coat a baking sheet with nonstick cooking spray or line with parchment paper. In a small bowl, whisk together egg white and 2 tablespoons olive oil. Lay a sheet of phyllo on the prepared baking sheet and, with a pastry brush, lightly coat surface with egg-white mixture. Sprinkle with 1 teaspoon breadcrumbs. Repeat this step, layering 4 more sheets of phyllo. Lay the final sheet of phyllo on top and brush with egg-white mixture. To form an edge to the tart, carefully roll over edges toward center, using the blade of a knife to help start roll.

With a rubber spatula, spread mustard over the surface of dough and sprinkle with cheese. (The tart can be prepared ahead to this point. Wrap and freeze for up to 2 months. Do not thaw before continuing.)

Arrange tomato slices on top in 5 rows of 8 slices each. Bake for 15 to 20 minutes, or until pastry is golden brown. Remove from oven and continue to let cook in the pan for 5 minutes. In a small bowl, combine basil, parsley and garlic. With fingers or a fork, dab some herb mixture onto each tomato slice. Slide tart onto a serving platter or, for bite-sized appetizers, slide it onto a cutting board and cut the tart into squares between the tomato slices with a sharp knife or pizza cutter. Serve warm or at room temperature. This recipe takes about 10 minutes to prepare and makes 40 appetizers.

INGREDIENTS

1 large egg white

2 tablespoons olive oil

6 (14x8-inch) sheets phyllo dough

5 teaspoons fine dry breadcrumbs

1/3 cup dijon mustard

1/4 cup freshly grated parmesan cheese

1 pound plum tomatoes, about 8, cored and sliced 1/4 inch thick

1 tablespoon fresh basil

2 tablespoons chopped fresh parsley

2 cloves garlic, finely chopped

SUBMITTED BY:
Barbara Knezovich, McKeesport

Ratatouille

DIRECTIONS

Preheat oven to 325 degrees. Heat olive oil in a large skillet. Crush or mince garlic, slice onion and add both to oil. Sauté until onion is transparent. While cooking onion, slice zucchini into rounds, cut pepper into strips and peel and cube eggplant. Dredge vegetables lightly in flour. Place onion and garlic into a Dutch oven or large casserole dish. Add more oil to the skillet, if necessary, and brown vegetables at medium-high heat. Add vegetables to onions. Cover and bake for approximately 1 hour. Finally, blanch and peel tomatoes and slice into mixture. Bake, uncovered, for another 30 minutes. Season with salt and pepper and add capers during last 15 minutes of cooking. Serve hot or cold with plenty of French bread.

INGREDIENTS

1/3 cup olive oil

2 cloves garlic

1 large onion

2 well-scrubbed zucchini

2 green peppers

1 small eggplant

3 tablespoons flour

5 ripe tomatoes

Salt and pepper, to taste

1 tablespoon capers

French bread, for serving

SUBMITTED BY:
Chris Fennimore, WQED Pittsburgh

America's
HOME COOKING

Raw Cauliflower and Gorgonzola Cheese Salad

Directions

Cut away core of cauliflower heads. Break each apart into individual florets. Holding florets with stems pointing up, thinly slice each one. Put the cauliflower into a large bowl and add cheese, parsley and basil.

Whisk together mustard and vinegar in a medium bowl. Whisk in olive oil a few drops at a time. Add garlic and season with salt and freshly ground pepper. (The dressing will taste strongly of vinegar. This will decrease during marinating.)

Add dressing to salad, cover and chill for 1 hour before serving. Serve on a bed of romaine lettuce. Serves 12.

Note

This salad can be made the night before.

Ingredients

2 medium heads cauliflower

1/2 pound gorgonzola cheese, crumbled

1/2 cup chopped parsley leaves

1/4 cup chopped basil leaves

Vinaigrette Dressing:

2 heaping tablespoons dijon mustard

1/2 cup white wine vinegar

1 1/4 cup olive oil

1 clove garlic, crushed

Salt and freshly ground black pepper, to taste

12 leaves romaine lettuce, for serving

Submitted by:
Susan Mihalo VanRiper, Allison Park

Roasted Asparagus

DIRECTIONS

Trim tough ends off asparagus and use a peeler to remove outer skin from the bottom half of each stalk. Blanch asparagus in boiling salted water for 2 minutes and shock in ice water, then drain. Toast breadcrumbs in a frying pan until golden brown.

Preheat oven to 350 degrees. Whisk together vinegar, lemon juice, mustard and a little salt and pepper. Slowly whisk in olive oil. In a large bowl or pan, mix asparagus with dressing, and then sprinkle with breadcrumbs. Spread asparagus out in a greased baking dish. Bake for about 15 minutes until heated through.

INGREDIENTS

1 pound fresh asparagus

1 cup fresh breadcrumbs

1 tablespoon balsamic vinegar

1 tablespoon lemon juice

1 teaspoon dijon mustard

Salt and pepper, to taste

4 tablespoons olive oil

America's
HOME COOKING

Roasted Broccoli and Cauliflower

DIRECTIONS

Preheat oven to 375 degrees. Cut cauliflower head in quarters and then use the tip of a chef's knife to carefully cut out core. Cut cauliflower florets to half the size of a golf ball.

Cut broccoli, trim florets from the stem and cut down to the same size as cauliflower. To prepare broccoli stems, peel off the tough and fibrous outside of the broccoli stem. (The inside of the stem is tender and delicious.) Cut it into chunks about half the size of the florets.

Keep broccoli and cauliflower separate—the cauliflower needs to cook a few minutes longer than broccoli does. If mixed together from the start, either the cauliflower will be undercooked or the broccoli will be overcooked.

Toss cauliflower in a mixing bowl with enough olive oil to generously coat the pieces. Sprinkle with salt, pepper and paprika. (Be careful about how much seasoning is used as the florets will soak up the oil and spices like a sponge.)

Spread cauliflower onto a cookie sheet with a rim, so the oil won't spill over the side. Place in oven for about 5 minutes while tossing broccoli with olive oil, salt, pepper and ginger in the same bowl used to season the cauliflower. Once cauliflower has cooked for about 5 minutes, add broccoli to pan and cook for an additional 12 minutes. Remove and serve immediately.

SUBMITTED BY:
Chef Jesse Sharrard, CorduroyOrange.com

INGREDIENTS

1 head broccoli
1 head cauliflower
Olive oil
Salt and pepper, to taste
Paprika, to taste
Ginger, to taste

Scalloped Tomatoes

DIRECTIONS

Preheat oven to 350 degrees. Cook onion in butter until tender, but not brown; stir in crumbled bread. In a 1-quart casserole, layer half of the tomatoes and sprinkle with salt, pepper and sugar. Cover with half of crumb mixture. Repeat layers. Bake, uncovered, for 30 minutes. Serves 6.

INGREDIENTS

1 medium onion, chopped (about 1/2 cup)

1/4 cup butter

3 slices bread, coarsely crumbled (about 2 1/4 cups)

6 medium tomatoes, peeled and sliced

Salt, to taste

Pepper, to taste

Sugar, to taste

SUBMITTED BY:
Reda Kirschman, Pittsburgh

America's
HOME COOKING

Slew

DIRECTIONS

In a medium-sized pot, heat oil and butter; sauté onion until transparent. Add tomatoes and cook for 5 to 10 minutes, allowing tomatoes to soften and release their juices. Add remaining vegetables and season to taste. Add enough water to allow mixture to steam. Cover pot and cook on low heat about 30 minutes or until vegetables are tender. Serves 4.

NOTE

This recipe is also good served over a bed of rice.

INGREDIENTS

2 tablespoons olive oil

2 tablespoons butter

1 medium onion, diced

1 quart tomatoes (about 6 to 8 medium tomatoes), peeled, seeded and cut into chunks

1 medium zucchini, sliced

2 to 3 potatoes, sliced

1 green pepper, diced

2 cups string beans

1 cup water

Salt and pepper

SUBMITTED BY:
Pauline Cleaver, Revloc

Spinach Salad

DIRECTIONS

Tear spinach into pieces in a big bowl. Mix all ingredients together just before serving.

NOTE

Serve a relish tray of celery and carrots with salad.

INGREDIENTS

1 bunch spinach, cleaned and drained well

2 (11-ounce) cans mandarin oranges, drained

1 medium red onion, thinly sliced

3 ounces crumbled feta cheese

Croutons

Freshly made Italian dressing mix

SUBMITTED BY:
Claire Hetrick, Butler

Stewed Tomatoes

DIRECTIONS

Remove stem end from each tomato; peel and cut into small pieces. In a medium saucepan, stir together all ingredients except bread cubes. Cover and heat to boiling; reduce heat and simmer 8 to 10 minutes. Stir in bread cubes and serve.

INGREDIENTS

3 large ripe tomatoes, about 1 1/2 pounds

1/3 cup finely chopped onion

2 tablespoons chopped green pepper

1 tablespoon sugar

1/2 teaspoon salt

1/8 teaspoon pepper

1 cup soft bread cubes

SUBMITTED BY:
Lola Olinski, Maynard

Stir-Fried Ginger Asparagus

DIRECTIONS

Snap tough ends from asparagus stalks and peel skin from the lower portions. Cut asparagus on the bias into 1-inch pieces. Heat oil in a skillet and add asparagus pieces. Add honey and ginger to pan and sauté until crisp-tender, about 2 to 3 minutes. Sprinkle with toasted pine nuts and serve. Serves 2.

INGREDIENTS

1/2 pound asparagus

1 tablespoon olive oil

1 teaspoon honey

1 teaspoon grated fresh ginger

1 tablespoon toasted pine nuts

America's
HOME COOKING

Sweet and Sour Brussels Sprouts

DIRECTIONS

Remove outer stems and trim bottom of sprouts. Cut a small "x" in the bottom of each sprout and steam in 1/2 cup salted water until just tender. Pour sprouts into a bowl of ice water to stop cooking and retain bright green color; drain. Meanwhile, in a large pan, sauté bacon until crisp. Remove bacon to a paper towel and reserve about 4 tablespoons of drippings. Turn heat to medium high. Add vinegar, sugar, salt and pepper. Stir to dissolve sugar and then add sprouts and keep stirring until glazed. Pour into a serving dish and sprinkle with crumbled bacon.

INGREDIENTS

2 pounds brussel sprouts

4 strips bacon

2 tablespoons cider vinegar

2 teaspoons sugar

1/2 teaspoon salt

Freshly ground black pepper

Sweet and Sour Green Beans

DIRECTIONS

Keeping bacon as a large slab, slice in opposite direction of bacon slices, to make 1/2-inch square pieces. (Bacon cuts easier when partially frozen). Separate pieces and place in a large frying pan. Cook bacon until slightly browned at medium-high heat, and then add onion rings. Cook mixture until the bacon is very crispy and onions are slightly browned, limp and translucent, stirring frequently, about 20 to 25 minutes. (Mixture will be dark.) Remove from flame for a few minutes and stir in vinegar and sugar.

Preheat oven to 325 degrees. Add onion/bacon mixture to green beans and mix carefully, taking care to not mash beans. Bake in oven, covered, for about 20 minutes or until hot. Mix and serve.

INGREDIENTS

1 pound regular-sliced bacon

1 very large yellow onion, cut in thick slices

2 (14 1/2-ounce) cans whole-cut green beans, drained

1/2 cup white vinegar

4 rounded tablespoons sugar

NOTE

Do not drain bacon and onion mixture. Mixture can be made up a day ahead and then refrigerated. Heat mixture to obtain mixable consistency and then add to green beans. Finish heating as noted above.

SUBMITTED BY:
Lori Walter, West View

America's
HOME COOKING

Swiss Chard, Beans and Tomatoes

DIRECTIONS

Thoroughly wash Swiss chard. Remove stems and tear remaining leaves into bite-sized pieces. Steam chard and onions in a large pot or wok with only the water that remains on the leaves after washing. When chard has collapsed, add tomatoes, olive oil, vinegar, garlic and shallots. Continue to steam for 5 to 8 minutes. Add beans with liquid and season to taste.

Serve with bread and thin slices of pecorino romano cheese. Serves 6.

INGREDIENTS

5 large bunches Swiss chard

2 medium onions, chopped

6 tomatoes, peeled, seeded and chopped

1/4 cup olive oil

1/4 cup balsamic vinegar

2 cloves garlic, crushed

2 large shallots, chopped fine

1 (16-ounce) can cannellini beans

Salt and pepper, to taste

Bread, for serving

Pecorino romano, sliced, for serving

SUBMITTED BY:
Susan Mihalo VanRiper, Allison Park

Tomatoes Oregonata

DIRECTIONS

Cut tomatoes into approximately 1-inch cubes. Crush garlic with the back of a knife and add to tomatoes along with the other ingredients. Stir with a wooden spoon and refrigerate for at least 4 hours. Serve with crusty French or Italian bread to soak up the juice that forms.

INGREDIENTS

6 medium tomatoes or 12 plum tomatoes

1 clove garlic

1/4 cup olive oil

1 1/2 teaspoons salt

1/2 teaspoon fresh black pepper

1 1/2 tablespoons oregano

1 tablespoon fresh basil, if available (optional)

French or Italian bread, for serving

SUBMITTED BY:
Chris Fennimore, WQED Pittsburgh

America's
HOME COOKING

Vegetable Bake

Directions

Preheat oven to 350 degrees. Mix first 6 ingredients (green beans through onion) well; place into a greased 9x13-inch baking dish. Mix breadcrumbs and melted butter or margarine together for topping; spread breadcrumbs over casserole. Bake for 20 minutes or until breadcrumbs are brown.

Ingredients

1 (14 1/2-ounce) can French-style green beans, drained

1 (15 1/4-ounce) can whole kernel corn

1/2 cup mayonnaise

1/2 cup shredded sharp cheese

1/2 cup chopped green pepper

2 tablespoons chopped onion

2 cups breadcrumbs

1/2 cup (1 stick) melted butter or margarine

Submitted by:

Catherine Monte Carlo, Monongahela

Zucchini Casserole

DIRECTIONS

In a skillet, melt butter and sauté onion until transparent, but not brown. Add ground round, salt and pepper; brown meat.

Put whole zucchini in a pot of water with 1 teaspoon salt and bring to a boil, boiling zucchini for 5 minutes. Remove from water, and cut into 1/4-inch slices.

Preheat oven to 250 degrees. In 2-quart casserole, layer meat, zucchini slices and cheddar cheese slices using half the ingredients. Repeat layers with remaining ingredients. Pour mushroom soup on top, directly out of can, and do not stir. Sprinkle top with cracker crumbs. Bake for 1 hour. Serves 4.

INGREDIENTS

2 tablespoons butter

1 medium onion, finely chopped

1 pound ground round

1/2 teaspoon salt

1/2 teaspoon ground pepper

3 medium zucchini, about 1pound

1 teaspoon salt

6 slices sharp cheddar cheese, about 6 ounces

1 (10 3/4-ounce) can cream of mushroom soup

1/2 to 1 cup saltine cracker crumbs

SUBMITTED BY:
Hazel-Lou Pryde, Kittanning

America's
HOME COOKING

Zucchini Fritters

DIRECTIONS

Mix all ingredients except flour and oil. Add flour and oil, and drop by teaspoonful into preheated pan with vegetable or olive oil. Lightly fry on both sides until golden brown.

INGREDIENTS

2 cups grated zucchini

1/2 cup grated romano cheese

1/2 cup freshly chopped parsley

2 eggs beaten

1 teaspoon salt

Dash pepper

3/4 to 1 cup flour

1 teaspoon oil

Vegetable or olive oil, for frying

SUBMITTED BY:
Joseph S. Certo, Forest Hills

Zucchini Parmesan

DIRECTIONS

Set out a 2-quart casserole and a 3-quart saucepan with a tight-fitting cover. Preheat oven to 350 degrees.

Wash, trim off ends and cut zucchini crosswise into 1/8-inch slices. In the saucepan, heat olive oil, and add zucchini with onions and mushrooms. Cover saucepan and cook zucchini mixture over low heat for 10 to 15 minutes or until tender, occasionally turning and moving mixture with a spoon. Remove zucchini mixture from heat; mix in half the grated cheese with fork. Mix tomato paste, salt, garlic salt/minced garlic and pepper, and pour into saucepan. Blend lightly and thoroughly; turn mixture into casserole and sprinkle with remaining cheese. Bake for 20 to 30 minutes.

INGREDIENTS

8 to 10 small zucchini squash, about 2 1/2 pounds

3 tablespoons olive oil

2/3 cup coarsely chopped onions

1/4 pound sliced mushrooms

2/3 cup grated parmesan cheese

2 (6-ounce) cans tomato paste, about 1 1/2 cups

1 teaspoon salt

1/2 teaspoon garlic salt or 1 clove garlic, minced

1/8 teaspoon pepper

SUBMITTED BY:
Vi Scaringi, Verona

America's
HOME COOKING

Zucchini-Tomato

DIRECTIONS

Remove ends of zucchini and cut zucchini into slices; sauté in olive oil. Add tomatoes, salt, pepper and garlic salt. Cook for about 6 to 8 minutes.

INGREDIENTS

2 medium zucchini

2 tablespoons olive oil

4 Roma tomatoes or 1 (28-ounce) can peeled plum tomatoes

1/2 teaspoon salt

1 teaspoon pepper

1 teaspoon garlic salt

SUBMITTED BY:
Peggy Fedak, McKees Rocks

WHAT'S FOR DINNER?
America's
HOME COOKING

STARCH

Andouille and Garlic Mashed Potatoes

DIRECTIONS

Chop andouille sausage finely and lightly brown in skillet over medium heat. Do not drain off oil.

Combine next 3 ingredients in a large pot; cover with water and bring to a boil. Cover, reduce heat and simmer for 20 minutes or until tender. Drain. Discard bay leaf.

Combine potato/garlic mixture, sausage, salt, pepper, chicken broth and butter, if needed. Mash by hand or with electric mixer on medium speed until well blended, but still chunky. Serve hot. Serves 6.

INGREDIENTS

1/2 pound andouille sausage

9 cups potatoes, about 3 pounds, peeled and cubed

10 garlic cloves, halved

1 bay leaf

3/4 teaspoon salt

1/4 teaspoon pepper

1 cup chicken broth

2 teaspoons butter (optional)

SUBMITTED BY:
Mark Bonsmann, Pittsburgh

115

Angelic Sweet Potatoes

Directions

Preheat oven to 350 degrees. Combine first 6 ingredients and mix well. Place in a 2-quart casserole pan. To make topping, combine all topping ingredients and mix well (topping will be crumbly). Sprinkle on top of potato mixture. Bake for 25 to 30 minutes.

Note

If serving a large crowd, this recipe can be doubled or tripled.

Ingredients

3 cups mashed, cooked sweet potatoes

1 cup sugar, preferably 1/2 cup white and 1/2 cup brown sugar

1/2 cup melted butter

1 egg

1/3 cup milk

1 teaspoon vanilla

Topping:

1/2 cup brown sugar

1/4 cup flour

2 1/2 tablespoons melted butter

1/2 cup chopped pecans or walnuts, optional

Submitted by:
Heidi and Monica Narr, Crafton

America's
HOME COOKING

Au Gratin Potatoes

Directions

Preheat oven to 350 degrees. Boil potatoes in salted water for 10 minutes; drain. Melt butter; blend in flour, salt and pepper. Add milk, and cook until thick. Stir in pimentos, onions, cheese, hot pepper sauce and potatoes. Turn potatoes into a 2-quart buttered casserole. Combine breadcrumbs and melted butter. Sprinkle on top. Bake for 30 minutes.

Ingredients

6 medium potatoes, peeled and diced

1/4 cup butter

1/3 cup flour

1 teaspoon salt

1/8 teaspoon pepper

2 cups milk

2 tablespoons pimentos, chopped

4 green onions, thinly sliced

6 ounces sharp cheddar cheese, grated

2 drops hot pepper sauce

1/2 cup breadcrumbs

2 tablespoons butter, melted

Submitted by:
Alyson Sprague, Sewickley

117

Baked Mashed Potatoes

DIRECTIONS

Peel potatoes and cut into 1-inch chunks. Boil until tender; drain. Preheat oven to 350 degrees. Mash potatoes and add 6 tablespoons of butter and then milk. Stir and whip until potatoes are smooth. Add mozzarella, romano cheese and salami. Stir to blend. Add salt and pepper. Use 1 tablespoon of remaining butter to grease the bottom and sides of a high-sided casserole dish. Coat bottom and sides with breadcrumbs. Spoon potato mixture into dish and dot the top with butter. Bake until top is golden brown.

NOTE

Be careful—this dish is very hot when it comes out of the oven!

INGREDIENTS

6 to 7 large potatoes

1/2 cup (1 stick) butter

1/2 cup milk

1/2 pound mozzarella, cubed

3 tablespoons grated romano cheese

1/8 pound hard salami, minced

Salt and pepper, to taste

1/2 cup breadcrumbs

SUBMITTED BY:
Chris Fennimore, WQED Pittsburgh

America's
HOME COOKING

Broccoli Corn Bake

Directions

Preheat oven to 350 degrees. Combine all but last 2 ingredients. Turn into 1-quart casserole. Mix remaining crackers and butter and sprinkle over casserole. Bake, uncovered, for 35 to 40 minutes. Serves 6.

Ingredients

1 (16-ounce) can cream corn

1 (10-ounce) package chopped frozen broccoli, cooked and drained

1 egg, beaten

2 cups coarsely crumbled butter crackers

1 tablespoon instant minced onion or 3 cups finely chopped onion

2 tablespoons butter or margarine, melted

2 teaspoons salt

Dash pepper

3 cups coarsely crumbled butter crackers

1 tablespoon butter or margarine, melted

SUBMITTED BY:
Chris Fennimore, WQED Pittsburgh

Champ

DIRECTIONS

Cook potatoes in a pot of boiling salted water until easily pierced with a fork. Bring cream and butter to simmer in heavy saucepan over medium heat, stirring often. Mix in green onions. Remove from heat and cover; let steep while potatoes finish cooking.

Drain potatoes thoroughly. Return potatoes to same pot and mash. Add cream mixture and stir until blended. Season dish, to taste, with salt and pepper.

NOTE

This recipe can be prepared 2 hours ahead. Cover and let stand at room temperature. Warm over low heat, stirring often.

INGREDIENTS

2 pounds russet potatoes, peeled and cut into 1-inch pieces

1/2 cup whipping cream

1/4 cup (1/2 stick) butter

1 bunch green onions, sliced, washed and trimmed (about 1 cup)

SUBMITTED BY:
Florence Ringeisen

America's
HOME COOKING

Confetti Rice Salad

Directions

Fluff rice with a fork and then add oil, vinegar, salt and pepper. Chop red and green pepper into a 1/8-inch dice. Peel and seed cucumber, and cut into a fine dice. Slice scallions into very thin rounds. Chop hard-boiled eggs coarsely. Toss chopped vegetables and chopped eggs with rice and chopped parsley. Garnish with grape tomatoes.

Ingredients

4 cups cooked rice

4 tablespoons olive oil

2 tablespoons white wine vinegar

Salt and freshly ground pepper, to taste

1 red pepper

1 green pepper

3 scallions

4 hard-boiled eggs

1 cucumber

1/2 cup parsley, chopped

1 pint grape tomatoes

Creamy Potato Bake

DIRECTIONS

Prepare mashed potatoes according to package directions, omitting butter. Add cream cheese, mix and heat well. Add egg, chives or onions (or both), and parsley flakes, and blend thoroughly. Preheat oven to 400 degrees. Transfer to a well buttered, 1-quart baking dish or soufflé dish. Dot mixture with 1 tablespoon butter and sprinkle lightly with paprika. Bake for 30 minutes.

INGREDIENTS

Instant mashed potatoes for 6

1 (4-ounce) container whipped cream cheese

1 beaten egg

2 tablespoons chopped dried chives or onions

1 tablespoon dried parsley flakes

1 tablespoon butter

Paprika, to taste

SUBMITTED BY:
Stephanie Matiak, Point Breeze

America's
HOME COOKING

Creamy Potato-Carrot Casserole

DIRECTIONS

In a medium saucepan, cook potatoes and carrots in boiling water for about 12 minutes, drain.

Preheat oven to 350 degrees. In a small skillet, cook bacon until crisp. Drain and crumble; set aside. In a large mixing bowl, mash potatoes and carrots with a potato masher or a mixer on low speed. Gradually beat in milk until mixture is creamy. Stir in eggs, parmesan cheese, green onion and sour cream or yogurt. Transfer to 1-quart casserole.

Bake, uncovered, for 20 minutes. Sprinkle casserole with bacon and 1 tablespoon parmesan. Bake an additional 15 minutes until center is set.

INGREDIENTS

2 cups peeled, diced potatoes, about 3/4 pounds

3/4 cup diced carrots

2 slices bacon

1/3 cup milk

2 eggs, beaten

1/2 cup parmesan cheese

1/4 cup sliced green onions

4 tablespoons sour cream or plain yogurt

1 tablespoon parmesan cheese, for topping

SUBMITTED BY:
Virginia M. Syrylo

Dolly's Spanish Rice

DIRECTIONS

Fry bacon until very crisp; drain off grease. Leave crumbles in pan and chop bacon into pieces and set aside. In the same pan, sauté green pepper and onions until soft. Return bacon to pan. Add tomatoes and seasonings. When all ingredients are incorporated, simmer for 20 to 25 minutes, stirring occasionally.

While sauce simmers, put 1 cup rice and 2 1/2 cups water in a 1-quart microwave bowl. Cook rice on high for 5 minutes and then on medium for about 16 to 20 minutes until all water is absorbed. (This also can be cooked on the stove top.) Add rice to simmering sauce. Simmer 10 more minutes and then serve.

INGREDIENTS

1 pound thick-cut bacon, chopped

1 green pepper, chopped

1 onion, chopped

1 (28-ounce) can crushed tomatoes

1 teaspoon garlic powder

1 teaspoon chili powder

Black pepper, to taste

1 cup converted rice (not instant rice)

2 1/2 cups water

SUBMITTED BY:
Twila and Patty Schulli, North Hills
(Recipe of Dolly Schulli)

America's
HOME COOKING

Easy Risotto

DIRECTIONS

Heat chicken stock in a saucepan until just boiling. Heat 1 tablespoon butter in another saucepan. Add onion and cook until it is softened, but not brown. Add rice and continue to cook for 1 minute, stirring to coat grains. Add wine and cook until it is almost completely evaporated. Add boiling chicken stock and stir until it comes back to the boil. Cover and reduce heat to a simmer. Every 4 minutes, remove cover and stir rice. Do this 3 times for a total cooking time of 16 minutes. Stir in cheese, remaining 2 tablespoons butter and black pepper.

INGREDIENTS

2 cups chicken stock

3 tablespoons butter

1 small onion, very finely chopped

1/2 cup arborio rice

1/4 cup white wine

1/2 cup grated parmigiano reggiano cheese

Freshly ground pepper, to taste

Fierce Potatoes

DIRECTIONS

Preheat oven to 400 degrees. Place potatoes in a large saucepan and cover with water. Cover and simmer for 5 minutes over reduced heat, drain. Combine potatoes, olive oil, thyme, salt and minced garlic in a large bowl, and toss gently to coat. Spoon mixture onto a 15x10-inch jelly roll pan sprayed with cooking spray. Bake for 15 minutes. Serves 8.

INGREDIENTS

2 pounds red potatoes, peeled and cut into 1-inch pieces

1 tablespoon olive oil

1 teaspoon dried thyme

1/4 teaspoon salt

1 garlic clove, minced

SUBMITTED BY:
Pat Robinson, Moundsville

America's
HOME COOKING

Hash Brown Casserole

DIRECTIONS

Preheat oven to 350 degrees. Mix first 5 ingredients together and pour into a greased 9x13-inch baking dish. Just before baking, crush corn flakes, mix with melted margarine or butter and spread on top of mixture. Bake for 45 minutes.

INGREDIENTS

1 (2-pound) bag frozen hash brown potatoes

1 (10 3/4-ounce) can cream of chicken soup

1 cup sour cream

1 teaspoon salt and pepper

2 cups shredded cheddar cheese

2 cups corn flakes

1/4 cup melted butter or margarine

SUBMITTED BY:
Catherine Montecarlo, Monongahela

Italian-Style Potatoes

DIRECTIONS

Preheat oven to 350 degrees. Peel potatoes and cut into 1/2-inch chunks. Fry in vegetable oil until golden brown. Remove potatoes and drain on paper towels. Pour off all but 2 tablespoons of oil. Sauté onion and peppers for 2 minutes. Add garlic and continue cooking until onions are wilted. Add spices and tomato sauce. Combine all ingredients and then add potatoes, tossing to coat with tomato and spices. Pour into a greased casserole dish and bake for 30 minutes.

INGREDIENTS

6 to 10 potatoes

Vegetable oil, for frying

1 large Vidalia or sweet onion

2 green peppers or 1 red and 1 green pepper

1 clove garlic, crushed

Oregano, to taste

Basil, to taste

Parsley, to taste

Salt and pepper, to taste

1 (8-ounce) can tomato sauce

SUBMITTED BY:
Chris Fennimore, WQED Pittsburgh

America's
HOME COOKING

Kathy's Red-Skin Ranch Potato Salad

DIRECTIONS

Mix all ingredients together. Stir gently; do not break potatoes. Salad should be prepared ahead of time and refrigerated to blend flavors.

INGREDIENTS

10 pounds red skin potatoes, boiled, cooled and quartered

1 pound bacon, diced, fried and drained

1 (16-ounce) bottle ranch salad dressing

1 bunch green onions, finely diced

Ground black pepper, to taste

Paprika, to taste

SUBMITTED BY:
Karen A. DeSimone, Pittsburgh

Lemon and Dill Orzo

DIRECTIONS

Heat oil in a saucepan; add onion and cook until wilted. Add orzo, white wine, chicken broth and thyme. Bring to a boil. Reduce heat to a simmer and cover. Cook for 15 minutes or until liquid is absorbed and pasta is tender. Stir in dill and lemon juice immediately before serving.

INGREDIENTS

1 tablespoon olive oil

1 small onion, finely chopped

1 cup orzo

1/2 cup dry white wine

1 1/2 cups chicken broth

1/4 teaspoon dry thyme

2 tablespoons chopped fresh dill

2 tablespoons lemon juice

America's
HOME COOKING

Mustard Mashed Potatoes

DIRECTIONS

Preheat oven to 350 degrees. Add sour cream, mustard, sugar and chives or green onions to mashed potatoes. Combine and place in a casserole dish. Bake for about 20 to 25 minutes.

To serve, top with additional chives or onions.

INGREDIENTS

1 cup sour cream

2 tablespoons yellow mustard

1 tablespoon sugar

4 tablespoons chopped chives or green onions

4 cups mashed potatoes, prepared with milk, butter, salt and pepper

SUBMITTED BY:
Sophia Gabler, Monroeville

Nutty Sweet Potato Nests

Directions

Preheat oven to 350 degrees. Combine sweet potatoes, sugar, spices and salt; mix well. Fold in 3/4 cup whipped topping. Divide mixture into 8 portions and shape into balls. Roll in nuts. Place on an ungreased cookie sheet. Indent centers with spoon to form "nests." Bake for 15 minutes. Fill centers with approximately 1/4 cup whipped topping or a small amount of miniature marshmallows, if desired.

Ingredients

2 (17-ounce) cans sweet potatoes or yams, drained and mashed

1/4 cup packed brown sugar

1/2 teaspoon cinnamon

1/4 teaspoon ginger cloves

1/4 teaspoon salt

1 (8-ounce) container whipped topping with real cream, thawed

1 1/4 cup chopped pecans or walnuts

Submitted by:
Dorcas Barney, Eighty-Four

America's
HOME COOKING

Old-Fashioned Potato Salad

DIRECTIONS

Stir all ingredients together to mix, cover and chill several hours before serving. Serve as is or in crisp lettuce cups.

For herbed potato salad, prepare as directed, but add 2 tablespoons minced fresh dill (or 1/2 teaspoon dill weed) and 1/2 teaspoon minced fresh marjoram (or 1/4 teaspoon dried marjoram).

INGREDIENTS

6 medium boiled potatoes, chilled, peeled and cubed

4 hard-cooked eggs, chilled, peeled and diced

1/2 medium sweet green pepper, cored, seeded and minced

1 medium yellow onion, peeled and minced

2 stalks celery, diced

1 cup mayonnaise

1/4 cup sweet pickle relish

1 1/2 teaspoons salt

1/8 teaspoon pepper

SUBMITTED BY:
Deborah Hilty, Harrison City

Oven-Roasted New Potatoes

DIRECTIONS

Wash potatoes and peel a stripe around the middle of each. Cook in gently boiling water for about 10 minutes. Preheat oven to 400 degrees. Drain and mix with butter, salt and pepper. Roast in oven until brown and tender. Sprinkle with parsley before serving.

INGREDIENTS

12 to 18 new potatoes about 2 inches in diameter

2 tablespoons butter

Salt and pepper

1 teaspoon chopped fresh parsley

America's
HOME COOKING

Parmesan Potato Puffs

DIRECTIONS

Preheat oven to 350 degrees. In a large bowl, thoroughly mix dry milk powder and water. Add potatoes, egg, salt, baking powder, pepper, onion, parsley and 1/2 cup cheese. Mix thoroughly.

Form mixture into 6 balls. On a plate, mix remaining cheese with almonds. Roll each ball in almond mixture to coat. Place on buttered baking dish. Bake for 30 to 35 minutes until puffed and lightly browned. Dust with paprika. Serves 6.

INGREDIENTS

1/3 cup instant nonfat dry milk powder

1/4 cup water

3 cups unseasoned mashed potatoes, about 4 to 5 medium potatoes

1 egg, beaten

1 teaspoon salt

1 teaspoon baking powder

1/8 teaspoon pepper

1/4 cup finely chopped onion

2 tablespoons chopped parsley

1 cup grated parmesan cheese, divided

1/2 cup chopped toasted almonds

Paprika, for garnishing

SUBMITTED BY:
Carol Waterloo Frazier, McKeesport

Pecan Sweet Potatoes

DIRECTIONS

Preheat oven to 350 degrees. Slice potatoes and put 1 layer deep in a greased 13x9-inch pan. Sprinkle with brown sugar, pecans and orange peel. Pour orange juice over top. Dot with butter and sprinkle with salt. Bake for 1 hour. Serves 8.

NOTE

This dish can be fixed ahead of time and refrigerated until ready to bake.

INGREDIENTS

6 medium sweet potatoes, cooked and peeled

1/2 cup brown sugar

1/3 cup chopped pecans

1 tablespoon grated orange peel

1 cup orange juice

2 tablespoons butter

1/2 teaspoon salt

SUBMITTED BY:
Regina M. Genter, Allison Park

America's
HOME COOKING

Perogie Casserole

DIRECTIONS

Cook noodles as directed. Sauté onion in butter. Mash potatoes with milk and 1/4 of cheese food. Layer in a 9x13-inch pan in the following order—onion and butter, noodles, potatoes and remaining cheese food. Repeat layer. Bake at 350 degrees, covered, for 15 minutes. Uncover and bake for 5 minutes.

INGREDIENTS

1 (12-ounce) package bow tie noodles

1 large onion

1/2 pound butter

5 to 6 medium potatoes, cut, boiled and cooled

Milk

1 (8-ounce) package pasteurized prepared cheese food

SUBMITTED BY:
Patty Roydes, Clinton Township

Potato Dumplings

DIRECTIONS

Mix salt, flour, nutmeg and baking powder.
Add slightly beaten eggs and flour mixture to
cooled mashed potatoes; mix. Drop mixture
by spoonfuls into rapidly boiling salted water.
Cook until dumplings rise to the top. Drain;
pour melted butter over dumplings to prevent
sticking. Sprinkle with minced parsley and
serve immediately. Makes 24 dumplings.

INGREDIENTS

1 1/2 teaspoons salt

1 cup flour

1/8 teaspoon nutmeg

2 teaspoons baking powder

2 eggs, slightly beaten

2 pounds cooked, mashed and
cooled potatoes, about 4 cups

2 quarts boiling water

2 teaspoons salt

Melted butter

Minced parsley, for garnishing

SUBMITTED BY:
Heather Rebic, Pittsburgh

America's
HOME COOKING

Potato Gnocchi

DIRECTIONS

Mix together potatoes, flour, garlic, salt, pepper and egg until a dough forms. Add enough flour to make a stiff dough. Knead until smooth and elastic.

Take a piece of dough about the size of a lemon and roll it out into a rope about the thickness of a pinky finger. Cut into 3/4-inch pieces. Form each piece into gnocchi by making a diagonal dent in the center and then rolling it along the tines of a fork. Gnocchi can also be left as small dumplings.

Drop 8 to 10 gnocchi into boiling salted water and cook for about 3 minutes. Dumplings will float to the top. Remove with a slotted spoon and keep warm while cooking remaining gnocchi in batches. Serve with melted butter, parsley and grated cheese, or with a thick tomato sauce.

INGREDIENTS

1 cup mashed potatoes
1 cup flour
1 clove garlic, mashed
1/4 teaspoon salt
1/8 teaspoon white pepper
1 egg, beaten

NOTE

If you don't want to cook gnocchi right away, put them on a floured cookie sheet and then in the freezer. After 1 hour or so, remove from cookie sheet and put in a plastic bag. Do not defrost before cooking.

SUBMITTED BY:
Chris Fennimore, WQED Pittsburgh

Potato Kugelis

DIRECTIONS

Preheat oven to 400 degrees. Peel and grate potatoes and onion with fine side of grater. Cut bacon into pieces, fry until crisp. Add bacon to potatoes along with milk, 3 beaten eggs and salt. Stir to mix well. Pour into greased pan. Bake for 15 minutes.

Reduce heat to 375 degrees, and bake 45 minutes longer. Serve hot with sour cream.

NOTE

The depth of the potato should be no less than 2 1/2 inches in the baking dish.

INGREDIENTS

10 large potatoes

1 medium onion

5 slices bacon

1/2 cup evaporated or regular milk

3 eggs, beaten

2 teaspoons salt

SUBMITTED BY:
Jonalyn Verna, North Huntingdon

America's
HOME COOKING

Potato Pancakes

DIRECTIONS

Shred potatoes and onion in a food processor or by hand using a cheese grater. Squeeze out excess moisture and mix together with other ingredients. Spoon into frying oil and fry lightly on both sides. Drain on paper towels.

INGREDIENTS

2 to 3 medium potatoes

1 small onion

1 egg

2 tablespoons flour

1 teaspoon salt

1/8 teaspoon pepper

Oil, for frying

Potato and Parmesan Gratin

Directions

Preheat oven to 400 degrees. Butter
13x9-inch baking dish. Layer 1/3 potatoes in
dish and sprinkle with salt and pepper. Drizzle
with 1/3 butter and top with 1/3 parmesan.
Repeat layers 2 more times. Pour milk evenly
over all. Bake potatoes for 15 minutes and
reduce heat to 350 degrees. Continue baking
until potatoes are tender and lightly browned
and most of milk is absorbed, usually about 1
hour. Let stand 1 hour before serving.

Note

These potatoes are especially good with
grilled veal chops.

Ingredients

2 1/2 pounds russet potatoes,
peeled and cut into 1/8-inch
slices

Salt and pepper, to taste

1/4 cup butter, melted

2 cups packed freshly grated
parmesan cheese

2 cups whole milk

Submitted by:
Robin DeFazio, Glenshaw

America's
HOME COOKING

Quick Cheese Noodles

Directions

Bring stock or bouillon to a boil. Add noodles and cook until tender and most of the liquid is absorbed. Add butter, cheese and milk; stir over low heat until cheese is melted. Season noodles with freshly cracked black pepper and salt.

Ingredients

2 cups chicken stock or 2 cups boiling water with 2 bouillon cubes, dissolved

1/2 pound elbow or other similarly small-shaped macaroni

1 tablespoon butter

4 slices American cheese

1/4 cup milk

Salt and pepper, to taste

Roasted Mustard Potatoes

DIRECTIONS

Preheat oven to 400 degrees. Spray a roasting pan 3 times to coat with vegetable oil. Put mustard, paprika, cumin, chili powder and cayenne pepper in a large bowl; whisk to blend Prick potatoes several times with tines of a fork and add to bowl. Toss to coat potatoes evenly. Pour coated potatoes into prepared roasting pan, leaving a little space between them.

Bake 45 minutes to 1 hour, until potatoes are fork tender. Serves 4.

INGREDIENTS

Light vegetable oil cooking spray

4 tablespoons Dijon mustard

2 teaspoons paprika

1 teaspoon ground cumin

1 teaspoon chili powder

1/8 teaspoon cayenne powder

16 baby red potatoes

SUBMITTED BY:
Nancy Polinsky (with credit to
Rosie Daley), WQED Pittsburgh

America's
HOME COOKING

Scalloped Potato Supreme

DIRECTIONS

Preheat oven to 375 degrees. Alternate layers of potatoes, green pepper and onion in greased 2-quart baking dish, season each layer with salt and pepper. Mix mushroom soup with milk, and pour over potatoes. Bake for 1 hour. Serves 8.

INGREDIENTS

8 medium potatoes, sliced

1/4 cup chopped green pepper

1/4 cup minced onion

2 teaspoons salt

Dash pepper

1 (10 1/2-ounce) can cream of mushroom soup

1 cup milk

SUBMITTED BY:
Regina M. Genter, Allison Park

Slovak Sour Potatoes

DIRECTIONS

Melt butter in a large skillet. Add flour and onions; brown well. Add stock and stir well to make a smooth sauce. Add bacon, parsley, lemon rind, lemon pepper seasoning and bay leaf. Simmer on low heat for 5 minutes. Add potatoes and vinegar. Cook for 15 minutes. Remove bay leaf. Taste for seasoning and add additional vinegar if necessary. Garnish with fresh parsley. Serves 4 to 6.

INGREDIENTS

4 tablespoons butter

3 tablespoons flour, preferably instant flour

1 medium onion, sliced or chopped

1 cup chicken stock, at room temperature

6 large cooked potatoes, sliced or cubed

2 slices bacon, fried and crumbled

2 teaspoons chopped parsley

1/2 lemon rind, zest or grated

1/2 teaspoon lemon-pepper seasoning

1/2 bay leaf

1 to 2 tablespoons vinegar, to taste

Fresh parsley, for garnishing

SUBMITTED BY:
Debbie Chuba, Johnstown

America's
HOME COOKING

Spanish Rice

DIRECTIONS

Heat oil in a saucepan. Add onion, garlic and rice; cook until onion is tender and rice is well coated with oil. Add chicken stock, oregano, salt or sazon goya, and chopped tomato. Bring to a boil. Reduce heat to a simmer and cover. Cook 18 minutes. Remove from heat and stir with a fork.

INGREDIENTS

1 tablespoon olive oil

1 small onion, chopped

1 clove garlic, minced

1 cup long-grain rice

2 cups chicken stock

1 teaspoon oregano

1 teaspoon salt or sazon goya

1 small tomato, chopped

Suzanne's O'Potatoes Casserole

DIRECTIONS

Prepare empty 4-quart or larger slow cooker by coating with oil or nonstick spray. Turn on to high setting. Wash potatoes and mushrooms; set aside. Slice cleaned onions first. Peel potatoes and put in ice water. Slice potatoes and return to ice water. Slice mushrooms last. Open both soup cans, and stir each to a spreadable paste—do not mix.

Layer ingredients into the preheated slow cooker in the following order—1/4 potatoes, 1/4 onions, 1/2 cheddar cheese soup, 1/4 mushrooms, 1/4 breadcrumbs and 1/2 soup can of water. Repeat layers, alternating the two soup flavors every other layer and seasoning each layer with fresh ground pepper. Put lid on slow cooker. Do not open while cooking.

If pot begins to boil before 2 hours, turn down to low. Cook for a total of 3 hours.

INGREDIENTS

8 cups sliced baby red potatoes

12 ounces sliced mushrooms

1 cup sliced yellow onions

1 (10 1/2-ounce) can cream of mushroom soup

1 (10 1/2-ounce) can cheddar cheese soup

1 cup seasoned Italian breadcrumbs

2 soup cans fresh water

Fresh ground black pepper, to taste

SUBMITTED BY:
Susan O'Neil, Pittsburgh

America's
HOME COOKING

Sweet Potato and Apricot Casserole

Directions

Preheat oven to 350 degrees. Cut apricots in quarters. Place sweet potatoes and apricots in a buttered 8x8-inch baking dish.

Mix sauce ingredients except for butter and bring to a boil. Remove from heat and add 2 tablespoons butter or margarine; pour over sweet potatoes and apricots. Sprinkle chopped pecans over sweet potatoes. Bake for 30 minutes.

Ingredients

1 (20-ounce) can sweet potatoes, drained

1 (15-ounce) can apricots, drained with juice reserved

Sauce:

3/4 cup brown sugar

1 1/2 tablespoons cornstarch

1/2 teaspoon cinnamon

1/2 cup orange juice

Reserved apricot juice

2 tablespoons butter or margarine

1/2 cup chopped pecans

Submitted by:
Julia Wovchko, Corapolis

149

Sweet Potato Custard

DIRECTIONS

Preheat oven to 450 degrees. Pierce sweet potatoes with a fork and bake on an aluminum foil-covered pan for 2 hours. Allow potatoes to cool enough to split open and scrape insides into a bowl. Lower oven temperature to 300 degrees. Blend in banana and milk until smooth. Add brown sugar, egg yolks and salt.

Spray a 1-quart casserole with nonstick cooking spray and add sweet potato/banana mixture. Bake for 30 minutes. Mix raisins, sugar and cinnamon, and sprinkle on top of casserole. Bake for another 15 to 20 minutes or until a knife inserted near center comes out clean.

INGREDIENTS

2 medium sweet potatoes

1 very ripe banana, mashed

1 cup evaporated skim milk

2 tablespoons packed brown sugar

2 beaten egg yolks or 1/3 cup egg substitute

1/2 teaspoon salt

1/4 cup raisins

1 tablespoon sugar

1 teaspoon ground cinnamon

Nonstick cooking spray

Sweet Potatoes with Sherry

DIRECTIONS

Preheat oven to 350 degrees. Mix all ingredients well, adding sherry to taste. Place in a lightly greased casserole dish. Bake for 30 to 45 minutes, until golden brown.

INGREDIENTS

4 cups sweet potatoes, cooked and mashed

1/4 teaspoon salt

1/2 cup sugar

1/2 cup black or regular walnuts

2 eggs, beaten

1/2 cup melted butter

1/4 to 1/2 cup medium dry sherry

SUBMITTED BY:
James Baran, Pittsburgh

Syrian Potato Salad

DIRECTIONS

Boil potatoes for 30 to 45 minutes. Cut
potatoes into small cubes. Combine potatoes,
parsley and purple onion into a bowl. Mix
together lemon juice and oil, and season with
salt and pepper. Add dressing to potatoes
and mix together; chill.

INGREDIENTS

10 potatoes

1 bunch parsley, chopped

1 medium purple onion, diced

1/2 cup lemon juice

1/4 cup oil

Salt and pepper, to taste

SUBMITTED BY:
Martha Abraham, Carnegie

America's
HOME COOKING

Yam and Cranberry Casserole

DIRECTIONS

Preheat oven to 375 degrees. Combine cranberries, sugar, orange slices, pecans, orange juice and spices in a 2-quart casserole. Bake, uncovered, for 30 minutes. Stir yams into cranberry mixture. Return to oven and bake until heated through, about 15 minutes. Serves 8.

INGREDIENTS

3 cups fresh, whole cranberries

1 1/2 cups sugar

1 small orange, sliced

1/2 cup pecan halves

1/2 cup orange juice

1/4 teaspoon nutmeg

3/4 teaspoon cinnamon

1/4 teaspoon mace

1 (40-ounce) can yams, drained

SUBMITTED BY:
Sharon Lemasters, Morgantown

WHAT'S FOR DINNER?

Index

*Recipes were prepared on "America's Home Cooking: What's for Dinner?"

Index

*Recipes were prepared on "America's Home Cooking: What's for Dinner?"

Index

Recipes were prepared on "America's Home Cooking: What's for Dinner?"

Index

America's HOME COOKING

Recipes were prepared on "America's Home Cooking: What's for Dinner?"